Will Greenwood was born in Blackburn in 1972 and was educated at Sedbergh School and Durham University. After graduating, he played rugby for Harlequins and Leicester Tigers, making his England debut in 1997. He went on to win 55 caps for England, scoring 31 tries. He was part of England's World Cup-winning and Grand Slam sides in 2003, and also went on three Lions tours. Since retiring from the game in 2006, he has worked as a pundit for Sky Sports and writes for the *Daily Telegraph*.

BULGARIAN BRUISES, BLOODGATE AND OTHER STORIES

THE CHANGING WORLD OF RUGBY

WILL GREENWOOD

SIMON & SCHUSTER

London · New York · Sydney · Toronto · New Delhi

A CBS COMPANY

First published in Great Britain as 'Will Greenwood on Rugby'
by Simon & Schuster UK Ltd, 2012
This paperback edition published by Simon & Schuster UK Ltd, 2013

A CBS company

1 3 5 7 9 10 8 6 4 2

material rep...   ...ublishers
woul...   ...rs

The articles in this book were first published in the *Daily Telegraph*

A CIP catalogue record for this book is available from the British Library

ISBN: 978-1-84983-716-3

Typeset by Hewer Text UK Ltd, Edinburgh
Printed in the UK by CPI Group (UK) Ltd, Croydon, CR0 4YY

To my wife Caro, my mum and old man, and to my children
Archie, Matilda, Rocco and of course Freddie, always with us

Contents

Introduction

I never dreamt I would become a rugby writer. When I daydreamed it was always about playing or scoring tries, never trying to make sense of a game that for many people is an unnecessarily complex way of getting hurt and muddy. At school rugby was a way to break up the days of studying, at university a means of making friends and drinking beer, and while I was working in London it became a way of letting off steam after a hard day in the financial markets. Professionalism seemed a long way off and not something I was actively preparing for, much like my eventual retirement from the sport.

Events have had a way of creeping up on me, forcing me to deal with even the most extraordinary things in a matter of fact way. You never think the good times will end and try to get through the difficult moments as quickly as possible. That's why I have so thoroughly enjoyed putting together this collection of articles. It has acted as a *de facto* diary, chronicling my life through rugby, reminding me of what I have done and lived through.

Whatever I may want to become in the future I can't get away from the fact that my past is stamped and was forged in the history of the game. I grew up in a rugby family and played the sport for the best part of three decades. It formed my view of life and ultimately shaped my career once I stepped off the field. During that time I have changed almost as much as the game. From a school-boy amateur to full-time professional, from a vehement hater of weight sessions to someone who understood that without them he would never succeed, from a player with an intuitive understanding of the game to a pundit who is paid to watch every game of each season and dig out key moments in the hope of sparking debate and catching the imagination of an increasingly hungry and demanding newspaper readership and TV audience. In much the same way that rugby players now jump from league to union, and from country to country, so I am now expected to be international in my approach, aware of what is happening in the southern hemisphere and the rest of the world as much as in the local clubs up and down the UK.

And if I have changed, then the game is almost unrecognisable. Upheaval has come so thick and fast over the past decade that many of the changes have been forgotten or blended into one. This collection has allowed me to curate not only my best writing and deal with jokes about how short that list would be, but also how the pieces are presented. Rather than following a strictly chronological timeline I have tried to break the book up into sections that show how the game has taken me places, how it has taught me key lessons from simple things such as passing to dealing with extreme pressure, and how its biggest personalities have had an effect on me. I have also focused on key events such as World Cups and big changes in the laws of the game.

Luckily, my job as a writer has also allowed me to move outside of rugby to experience other sports and see if there are any common threads that unite athletes the world over, or if there are any truths that can be imported back into the game to help make it better. I found this to be one of the most enjoyable parts of the process because there is no doubt that rugby is still developing both as a game and a business. The more it can learn the stronger it will become. And this, in the end, is what I hope this collection will show the reader; that the sport can change and evolve, providing a bright future for all of us who love it and live it every day.

PART ONE

Rugby Can Take You Places

From Bulgaria to Buckingham Palace, rugby can take you places you never thought you'd get to. And I mean mentally as well as physically. I've met sporting legends and held hands with injured soldiers and some of Britain's most troubled kids. A rugby tackle nearly killed me and on another occasion left me crying in pain with a dislocated shoulder but the game still managed to help dry my tears when personal tragedy hit home. And when it came time to retire from a game I loved, rugby showed me that there was more to life than what happened on the field. Rugby has been central to my life and has given me more than I ever expected. It's been the journey of a lifetime.

Rugby Can Take You To Hell And Back

Thanks to everyone for the memories

In 2006, I realised that my time as a professional rugby player was coming to an end and I made the big decision to retire. It wasn't easy, especially as I wasn't sure what life outside of sport would hold in store.

Old centres never die, they just lose their pace and stop attacking the gain line. As hard as it has been for me to admit, the time has come to retire from the game that has always been part of my life. I understand the reasons. I'm getting slower – if that were possible. I can no longer perform to the levels I would wish, and my body is falling apart; six operations, broken bones, a near-death experience, torn ligaments, dislocated shoulders and hamstrings tighter than guitar strings.

Other people have fared worse, but for me this is enough. My brain can still see the options, I just can't seem to put them into action. Part of my unwillingness to admit the inevitable has been a fear of what the future might hold.

On July 1, I will not be climbing into the car and heading off for pre-season training. On Saturdays I will not lose my appetite to pre-match nerves. My kit bag will be put up into the loft, only getting dusted off for the odd game of five-a-side football.

I need to focus on different areas of my life, and the change will not be easy. Rugby is part of my DNA.

My mum used to take me to games when I was smaller than the ball, and it remained a family affair. I played rugby with my dad at Preston Grasshoppers, warming up with a schooner of sherry and then watching him hunt down anyone who tackled me late. I remember my mum's face after I won my first England cap, and her expression when Dad said I could keep playing in a school match if I used his scarf to hold the broken collar-bone in place and stood at full-back. (He still reckons I came off too easily and should have stayed to kick the goals.)

For a Blackburn lad who was only ever after a runaround with the lads, rugby has taken me on one hell of a journey. I have ended up in Ghana, New Orleans, Fiji and even Buckingham Palace. I have soared to the peaks and slumped into the troughs. You don't always win, you don't always play well. In the end, it really doesn't matter. What counts is the feeling of unity that being part of a team brings.

A lot of people want to know what happens in an international changing room. To be honest, there is very little difference between England's and the others dotted around the nation on any given weekend. Every team has a head-banger, a thinker, a smiler, a scary bastard. Every coach passes on his final thoughts and secretly crosses his fingers. After the game there is one player who is always last out of the changing room, one who dodges the ice bath, and another who ramps up the music.

There are no secret rites, you do not discover the meaning of life. What you have to do is learn to trust, share your hopes and fears, and show you are ready to put your body on the line. These are the bonds that are so much harder to replicate in the real world over a cup of coffee. It will not be the games I hanker after, but the changing room.

Memories both good and bad, like Durban after winning the Lions series in 1997, and Auckland when we had lost a series 3-0.

In Sydney on that famous night, but also in Paris in 1999 when our World Cup fell apart. At the Stoop and at Welford Road, winning trophies and getting relegated. Oddly, my memories are often stronger in times of failure than in victory. The changing room was always a home away from home, and in times of family tragedy it even provided sanctuary.

When my wife, Caro, and I lost our little baby boy, Freddie, in September 2002, rugby seemed the last place I could find peace. Yet the lads of both Harlequins and England allowed my mind to relax for brief moments. At the World Cup in 2003 when it seemed we were going through the whole terrible process again, rugby gave me a respite. It allowed me to keep breathing, keep living.

I still remember the phone call before England's crunch game against South Africa, when Caro told me she was being rushed into an emergency operating theatre. Clive Woodward – who gave me my chance at international level and whose loyalty went beyond the call of duty – booked me on every available flight out of Perth. In the end I stayed and played, heading back to the UK after the final whistle. During the match I even scored a try and if you watch the replays you can see a smile on my face, because for a short time rugby had pushed the worry from my mind. There are not many jobs you can say that about.

Caro has been the greatest partner and wife I could have wished for, insisting on my return to rugby after we lost Freddie, not asking me to stay with her when we risked losing our second son, Archie, and demanding we make a pact: she would stay in hospital, only if I promised to go back to Australia and come home with the World Cup.

What will be strange is that she has only ever known me as a rugby player. But if she hopes to have me around the house immediately, she may end up disappointed. I still have two months of rugby left, two months as part of a squad who stuck together with their fans and their board, and refused to crumble after relegation.

Harlequins should be immensely proud of themselves. The fans deserve Premiership rugby at the Twickenham Stoop and should that happen, it will be one of my happiest memories. There have been others. Jumping up and down with Wilko after winning the World Cup; organising two black-tie charity balls in memory of Freddie and seeing all my rugby mates there; scoring a hat-trick against Wales surrounded by men like Mike Catt, Austin Healey and Iain Balshaw. I will never forget laughter in the scariest of moments, like the time Mike Tindall and I were under the cosh in Wellington, with only six forwards left on the field, and the message coming from the touch-line to tackle. It has been a privilege to stand shoulder to shoulder with team-mates for more than a quarter of a century.

Of all the magical performances, there are two that stand out, because the individuals involved almost achieved what every player strives for – the perfect 80 minutes. Both were in 2003, neither was at the World Cup. The first was a Grand Slam decider at Lansdowne Road, when Jonny Wilkinson was magnificent. A man who leaves nothing to chance, he was awe-inspiring that day. We had our tactical differences, but after that match I vowed to always back him up. If he was willing to put that much effort in for a team then the rest didn't matter.

The second performance was put in by a man who I cannot hold in higher regard, Martin Johnson. Pound for pound, eyebrow for eyebrow, finger point for finger point, the greatest captain and player you could find. Leading England to victory over the All Blacks in Wellington, Johnno went closer to the perfect game than anyone. On that blustery night he was The Man, leading from the front, grabbing the game, and anyone within his reach, by the scruff of the neck.

The one thing that Johnno knew better than anyone was when to call it quits. It's right to follow his lead one last time. I've been lucky to straddle the amateur and professional era. There is a certain poetic symmetry to a former HSBC trader who used to leave work early for training and never imagined getting paid to play rugby now having to get his kicks in a suit.

It won't be easy, and I'd be lying if I said I wasn't nervous. My life in rugby has been great. Thanks to everyone for the memories.

Will Greenwood factfile

DOB: 20.10.72
Born: Blackburn (father Dick, former England flanker and coach)
Age: 33
Clubs: Harlequins, Leicester
England debut: v Australia 1997 (one of five new caps selected by Clive Woodward)
Caps: 55
Tries: 31
Last capped: Australia 2004 (rep)
Lions tours: 1997 South Africa, 2001 Australia, 2005 New Zealand (two caps)

The healing properties of sport

When Darren Clarke gave a heroic display to help win the 2006 Ryder Cup after the death of his wife, it got me thinking about the healing powers of rugby and sport in general. Sport had helped me through the most difficult time in my own life . . .

Sport has incredible properties. The ability to unite, to entertain, to give hope. When you see Trafalgar Square crammed with thousands of people waiting patiently to see a bunch of guys who had been throwing a pig's bladder around in Australia, you realise how powerful it can be. I'll never forget the scenes in London in 2003, which showed us how much England's Rugby World Cup victory meant.

Other stirring moments that come to mind include Michael Vaughan and his men at the Oval beating the Australians, and Kelly Holmes' face as she crossed the line seemingly unsure of whether she had won Olympic gold while the rest of the country was screaming at the TV in utter delirium. Or listening to Garry Herbert talking us through those final strokes as Pinsent and Co. triumphed by the smallest of margins at Athens 2004. Total drama for all concerned, theatre the like of which you could not script.

The 2006 Ryder Cup was no different, as I was glued to a television from 8 a.m. on the Friday until just after 6 p.m. on Sunday watching a team so united, so at ease, so confident in their own ability. The European Ryder Cup team were a force of nature, a wave of blue that swept across the scoreboard and would not be halted by any American counter-attack.

Whenever the US looked like coming back at us Ian Woosnam, the tiny Welshman, galvanised his troops, sent them back out in different groups and they simply went about hammering more nails into the Americans' hopes.

But even in this gladiatorial sporting arena, when the best of the best went toe to toe, one man stood tall above it all. Darren Clarke. A giant of a man both physically and emotionally. You can do nothing but doff your cap to him, admire him, support him and thank him.

Clarke has been part of something truly special and played his role majestically – to see him hugging Woosnam, to see him spraying Lee Westwood with champagne and to listen to him talking so enthusiastically about what the whole week had meant to him, was inspiring.

Sport has another hugely important property, and to me its healing ability is its greatest. When you find yourself in a dark place, when you feel there is no joy left in you, when you are unsure what you will do with the rest of your life – summarised so beautifully by the poet W H Auden: 'Stop all the clocks, cut off the telephone, Prevent the dog from barking with a juicy bone' – it is difficult to know where to turn. But you can turn to sport.

Out in the arena, surrounded by friends and doing what you have always done, you find yourself living again, you can breathe more easily, you can smile a smile that you thought had left you forever, there is hope. The dark days will always be there, there will be times when you struggle to understand why something has happened. When you have lost someone who was part of you, there will always be a part of you missing, but healing starts with those first few smiles, those first few tentative steps taken with your trusted friends, and sport allows you to take them.

I cannot, of course, begin to understand what those few weeks were like for Darren Clarke after the death of his wife. I can only tell you of my own experience. My wife and I found the incredible healing properties of sport so comforting in dealing with our own grief after the death of our baby boy, Freddie. Out on the field or on the course, where you are asked to perform at the highest level – where in my sport huge men are trying to knock you into next week, where in golf the opposition are trying to apply pressure that they hope your game will not be able to endure – you enter a world of calmness, a world you truly understand, a place that allows for brief moments to escape reality and return to childhood innocence, for we all took up our sport for fun and enjoyment, the rest was always a bonus.

Your thoughts always return to your loved ones when the action is calm but when called upon, your mind returns to its state of calm and well-being as the battle for victory ensues. It is only when it is over, when the game is won, that the emotion sweeps over you again, but there is no better place in the world to be than among your friends, surrounded by those with whom you have achieved Herculean glories.

I am not foolish enough to try to describe how Darren Clarke truly felt; I can only say how humbled I was by his performance – not as a golfer, but as a husband and a father. The whole sporting world salutes a true hero and hopes that, given time, he will find happiness again. Sport is a true healer.

The deadly side of the game

Not everyone has a photo of themselves on the day they nearly died. I do, and it still creeps me out.

I was so young, I look so scared. Every time I see that photo I am convinced I knew something was about to happen. It just does not look like me.

I am not a joker before games, but I like to think I never forget to smile. Not on that day. I was in Bloemfontein in South Africa with the 1997 Lions. The only uncapped player, living a dream and getting ready for the unofficial fourth Test against the mighty Free State.

My parents had just flown over and we met in the hotel before the game. They got the photo taken, Mum on one side, Dad on the other, and they still have it up in their house in North Wales. None of us knew that a few hours later I would be close to death and they would be out of their minds with worry.

We were still enjoying the occasion because that trip to South Africa was the greatest tour of my life. The midweek team had a riot in 1997, we never looked like losing.

The victory against the Gauteng Lions (formerly Transvaal) at Ellis Park, the home of South African rugby, is seen as the turning point of the tour. A week before, the likely Lions Test side had been buried by Northern Transvaal in Pretoria.

We needed something special in the stadium where South Africa had been crowned world champions two years earlier. John Bentley scored 'that try', where he turned them inside out, and the Test team came into the changing room after the game and celebrated as if we had won the series.

On a Lions tour, you cannot over-estimate the importance of unity and togetherness. It was onwards and upwards from there. The first-Test victory on June 21 stunned the world, and the dummy from Matt Dawson on the way to his crucial try still stuns me. And so it was, that our turn came around again, and Free State were lining up to give us a smashing.

The Lions team meeting was unbelievable. Lions' coach Jim Telfer, even writing his name has the hairs on the back of my neck standing up, gave us a speech that few could match. Then on to the bus, and the arrival at the dark, brooding concrete stadium. Barbecues everywhere, and quickly we were into the lair, into the changing room.

South Africa were relying on the Free State boys to dent the physicality and psychology of the now rampant Lions. I still remember arriving at my peg and thinking there had been a terrible mistake. I never wear No 12. But as an uncapped player you say nothing, as a youngster playing alongside Allan Bateman, one of the finest exponents of outside-centre play of the last generation, you keep quiet.

I loitered in the changing room that night. You don't get many chances to be in such an elite environment and I didn't want to waste it warming up.

Ollie Redman was captain that night; I couldn't believe how hairy he was, everywhere except on his head. Strange memories. Then Batman, as we called Allan, returned from his usual Olympic warm-up, and wandered over to his young sidekick, me, and said words that will live with me forever.

'Don't cut your sleeves off tonight, there is a bit of dew on the grass and the long sleeve will help your grip of the ball.'

An absolutely correct and valid point but one that would almost end my life. 'Wonderwall', the tour song, as always blared out during the warm-up, and we were ready. Free State never saw it coming.

We absolutely destroyed them in that opening half. The game was over by half-time and so was my tour. Mike Catt had opened holes all over the place that evening, and I was enjoying some nice easy yardage up the middle from simple scissors moves.

It was all lined up again, and I set off on the switch and found space. But as I looked to stretch away, Jaco Coetzee, the Free State No 8 just caught the sleeve I should have cut off. There was nothing illegal in what followed. Rough, but not foul play. I was 12 stone dripping wet and he put a fire out with me, swinging me round and throwing me to the floor, my arm pinned to my side by that bloody sleeve.

The rest, I am afraid, I have had to put together down the years by watching the incident on tape and talking to old pals. Because the next thing I really remember is being in Durban for the second Test four days later. By all accounts, things had gone very wrong very quickly on the pitch.

Austin Healey was straight over to me, sensing something was seriously wrong, gum shield whipped out, stuffed down my sock, and turned on my side. The doctor, James 'Robbo' Robson, was on in a flash.

My mum nearly followed. She was sprinting down the steps and was about to charge on to the field when Jason Leonard pulled off one of the great last-ditch tackles.

'Come here Mrs Greenwood, there is nothing you can do, he is in good hands, let's just get him off the field first.' He saved me from total humiliation – a mother on the pitch in the middle of a Lions series.

Slow and methodical, Robbo controlled the medical staff as they lifted me on to the stretcher. The faces looked pale carrying me off.

As we passed my mum, she cried: 'William, William, what have you done?'

It is not a video I want to see again, and I now understand how hard it is for mothers across the country to watch their children take the field worrying if they are going to be hurt. The anguish was etched on her face. In later meetings, the good doctor said he thought I had gone. The video of the medical room shows me all I needed to know. Robbo was white and shaking, my mum was distraught in the background.

I had swallowed my tongue, my pupils were not reacting to light, my throat was about to be cut open to free up the airways. I can tell you that there was no out-of-body experience, no going towards the light. I just wasn't going to wake up.

Then it happened. With Robbo's help and my mum's howls I came to.

What was the first thing I did? I told my mother to go away as she was embarrassing me.

I was transferred to the ambulance, my old man accompanied me. I was asleep again, the body shutting down to recover. Then suddenly, the journey had hardly begun when I sat bolt upright and shouted 'Dad, tell them it's my hamstring'.

As soon as I had said it, I was straight back down and asleep. You see in those days, concussion was a mandatory three-week ban, and my old man had always told me never to admit concussion.

Somewhere in the dark recesses of my mind I must have known it would end the tour I wanted to go on forever. I still smile at that. I am still proud that my battered brain was still thinking. At the hospital, I was given brain scans and a bed. I rang my wife. She tells me we chatted for an hour. I don't remember a word, and maybe my inability to listen began that night.

I have one hazy memory of that time. I woke again at 4.30 a.m.

and all I could hear was Afrikaans, I had no idea where I was. I lifted my sheets and was still in full Lions kit, gum shield down my sock. I thought I was dreaming. Confused or not, I was not hanging around in that hospital, no matter how messed up my head was.

The second Test was three days away. I headed down to Durban and my memories began to flood back. Rooming with Nick Beal, the glorious beach and then that amazing night, high up in the stands as we watched Neil Jenkins kick South Africa to the brink and then the Jerry Guscott drop goal that sealed it.

On the pitch, scenes that no matter how hard I bang my head I will never forget. The stuff of legend. My drinking ban ignored, it was one of the great nights. I have realised in later life just how close I was to losing everything. But would I turn back the clock and miss that tour? Are you bloody crazy?

Those were the days of our lives, my friend, and a Lions tour is a once-in-a-lifetime opportunity. It is the memory of what was achieved in 1997 that makes all the pain and risk worthwhile.

No pain, no gain?

Having shoulder problems as a rugby player has nothing to do with position or size. I had four shoulder operations, the first as a 20-year-old in 1993, and my final one in the spring of 2005 at the age of 32.

The odd thing about your shoulder popping is that it makes almost no sound. It is like a slide and stretch, followed by shock, pain and bewilderment.

You realise you are badly injured. You know it's all over, not just for an afternoon but for weeks to come. There is the strange sensation of having a bone protruding and putting pressure on skin in a way the body just doesn't recognise.

And then there is the pain. The body desperately wants everything back in its socket, and everything around the joint spasms.

If you think it is hard to dislocate a shoulder, it is nothing compared to putting it back in again. As the spasms and pain come, so the shoulder becomes trapped in its new surroundings. That's why doctors and physios try to manipulate it back in immediately on the pitch. The longer the shoulder is out, the more damage is done to the surrounding ligaments.

My first dislocation happened while I was playing against Oxford University at Iffley Road.

Audley Lumsden stepped inside my outstretched arm, the classic way an outside back would dislocate a shoulder; my body going one way, the arm the other, with a player hitting the middle at full tilt.

A doctor in tweed and wellies took me into the old changing shed, asked me to lie on my back, removed a boot, placed a woolly socked foot under my armpit and yanked for all he was worth.

The tears rolled down my cheeks, I held back a scream. And then, under the traction of his foot, the pop came as the vacuum was filled, the shoulder slotted back in its place. I had a masochistic realisation that the pain I had just endured was worth it.

They use more subtle techniques now, not requiring traction or brute force. No matter, because this is just the first step. Next comes the wait for the specialist for his view on your injury. England use

Len Funk for the Northern boys and Andrew Wallace for the lads down South.

The most likely course of action is a MRI arthrogram – where they scan you after injecting a blue dye into the joint to check the leakage from the socket and gauge the damage and potential style of surgery. Once this is done, you go under the knife.

There are different types of shoulder surgery and I have had three of them. In 1993 it was a Bankart lesion repair, where your muscles and ligaments are used to keep the ball and socket secure.

In 1998 I had the capsular shrinkage approach where the socket is shrunk to a snug fit using extreme heat once the bone, or ball, is back in place. Finally, in 2004 and 2005, I had the slap lesion repair (superior labral tear from anterior to posterior), still widely used.

In this process they try to re-attach the labrum with darts to the rim of the socket from where it has been torn away.

Gone are the days of the full anaesthetic, which put you into a blissful sleep but left you groggy for days. Now you are awake with a numb arm and shoulder. And instead of the big scars that opened you up to the world, today's injured get it all done through cuts, arthroscopies, that look like shaving nicks.

The best bit is when they drill your shoulder and then attach the darts. You smell burning bone and experience the sensation of a power tool working away inside you. You think it can't get worse at that point, yet it does.

Welcome to the sling. Four weeks of doing nothing lest you cause more damage. Remember that no matter how small the external scars, inside it's akin to a car crash. You get to take your arm out of the sling every now and then.

Then after a month, the work begins. Mighty men are reduced to lifting one-kilogram dumbbells. Giant elastic bands are attached to home radiators and car doors. Internal rotations, external rotations, you are retraining the arm to work. It's not about the big muscles in the early days, it's the little ones.

Slowly they begin to let you loose, running and weightlifting after about eight weeks, and then, at about 10 weeks, maybe hold a pad in training, the gradual reintegration into full training. Finally, if all has gone well, three months after the operation you find yourself in boots and gum shield, the referee's knock and you're back out there again.

No matter how you have prepared, nothing can replicate that moment when an opponent takes on the shoulder that a while back could not even lift a cup of tea. The hit comes, you wait, nothing happens. You get up, dust yourself down, shoulder still attached, and off you go.

The sobering thought for the current crop of injured, though, is that things will never seem the same. The scars will remind you every time you look in the mirror.

Rugby Can Introduce You To A Few Choice Characters

Rugby is a game of character for characters. From the hard, silent men in the pack to cheeky, chatty scrum-halves, the game has them all. I've had the privilege, or rather misfortune, to have met quite a few. They have punched me on the nose and run round me, they've laughed at my skills and been shut up by defeat, they've stood next to me when it mattered and never let me down. What's more, they've all stayed in my memory. Rugby has also given me the chance to meet some of my sporting heroes and learn one or two skills from pros in other sports. From darts to horse riding, rowing to race yachting, I have had a crack at them all. Luckily I am still here to tell the tale.

The best spanner thrower around

As the sand wedge hurtled through the air, making a noise akin to a helicopter's rotor blade and with the clear intent of wounding someone, I wondered how on earth a quiet game of golf could have come to this.

The day had started well. It was Richmond golf course, 48 hours before England were due to play New Zealand in the group stages of the 1999 Rugby World Cup. A friendly fourball had set off with Austin Healey and Will Greenwood representing the Leicester Tigers, Matt Dawson and Nick Beal the Northampton Saints.

By the time we made it to the 14th hole, it was clear the Tigers were going to carry the day and nerves were getting frayed. As Matt Dawson lined up a putt that could have kept his game alive, Austin decided it was time to discuss the state of play. That's the trouble when you pit two of the world's most competitive men against each other – they just can't help it.

A couple of comments was all it took, but the fuse had been lit. The fireworks came on the 15th when Austin found a bunker and was accused of cheating by Dawson. 'Call me a cheat once more and I will knock your head off,' threatened an irate Austin, who to this day swears he never flattened the sand behind his ball.

It was too good an opportunity to miss for Dawson, a player who is always happy to press other people's buttons on the field, and he once more accused Austin of cheating. No more slow fuse, the explosion was sudden and the golf club flew through the air as Austin charged out of the sandpit, took his glove off and squared up.

Luckily good sense and humour prevailed, and we all fell about laughing. But Dawson had once again shown one of his true, and very handy, skills – the wind-up. I tell you, play that man at Cluedo and you can guarantee that the lead piping would get involved before too long. Dawson has been involved in some titanic battles in his illustrious career against foes including the likes of George Gregan, Justin Marshall, Robert Howley and Joost van der Westhuizen. They have all had to deal with the constant chatter, the persistent haranguing, the deadly step that has done many like a kipper, the sixth sense that puts Dawson in the right place at the right time, and, as was so beautifully illustrated on the golf course, his ability to find a chink in an opponent's armour and pick at it until it becomes unbearable. And while he may not be the one to toss his golf clubs into the air, Matt Dawson is the best spanner thrower around.

The real Shaggy

I had my first argument of the Lions tour within an hour of meeting up with Shane Horgan. We have had a long-standing dispute, you see, because both of us have been called Shaggy for a long time and both of us have been trying to get rid of the nickname for a long time.

While Shane is certainly one of the scruffiest wings and not one of the quickest, lolloping around at about six foot four inches tall, appearances can be deceptive. He lost the argument, by the way, and was stuck with the nickname on tour – and I became Will again – and anyway it's a long time since Shaggy relied on his speed.

Horgan is a tremendously articulate and intelligent bloke with an appetite for travel and debate. Along with Denis Hickie and Gordon D'Arcy, he was one of the great coffee-drinking thinkers on the Lions tour.

On the pitch and off he was one of the top performers, marked out by his consistency, endeavour and ability to find space. He also is a very humble guy, the least known of the Leinster triumvirate of Brian O'Driscoll, D'Arcy and himself.

Quick blokes tend to snatch headlines. They are the guys whose feet twinkle that little bit faster, who can accelerate through half a hole before you even see it. When they have the ball, the crowd rises. Such excitement does not follow Horgan around. Where this Leinsterman beat everyone was in the brain department.

Horgan was one of the most telling contributors to Irish rugby in recent years, and he was a man who – dare I say it – has occasionally been missed more than 'yer man' himself, O'Driscoll. When Horgan played well, Ireland played well. He was a creator of space, he was always thinking two moves ahead on the rugby chess board. While Shane is a big bloke who you ignore at your peril when he trucks it up the middle, he also has tremendous footballing skills.

Against England in the 2006 Six Nations, he gave his audience a little bit of everything. For the first try he did what every poacher does best, he anticipated an error, he took a gamble that something might happen.

The English drift defence had marshalled the Irish midfield well, O'Driscoll looked for some territory and nudged the ball ahead with a kick to a well-positioned Ben Cohen. Then came the error – a combination of oval ball and a misplaced foot – and quick as a flash Shane was on it. One chance, one try. Shaggy then waited; he roamed, he carried, he tackled.

The excitement followed others while he quietly went about his business tracking the ball, biding his time, waiting for a chance. In truth he should never have been given the opportunity to show off his skills.

England gave Ireland a chance to win by running a back peel at a line-out and losing possession in the middle of the pitch. England were on the rough side of some calls all day, but this was one call all of their own making.

The ball should never have left the bottom right-hand corner of the field. England's pack were in the process of dismantling the Irish eight in those final minutes. Andy Goode should have been in his armchair sipping man-of-the-match champagne. At this level you make your own luck. Ireland certainly did in those final seconds.

Ronan O'Gara dinks a chip in behind the England backs, Tom Voyce gambles and misses, and O'Driscoll is off. He thinks about going on the outside, but Cohen does his job in defence; the split-second means Horgan must break stride to take the pass.

This buys just enough time for Lewis Moody to make the first of two wonder tackles, but rather than die with the ball and go for the corner Horgan stays away from the touchline and has the strength to recycle the ball with three Englishmen all over him.

The ball goes left, Shane is back on his feet, back into position and does what he does best; he loiters with intent. Seconds out, round two of Moody versus Horgan. Peter Stringer floats a wonderful ball over the top, and with a combination of strength, footwork, intelligence and experience, Horgan just gets the better of Moody's attempt to tackle him into touch. What a reach, what a try! What a footballer!

Brains and brawn

During the 2007 Six Nations Nick Easter won his first cap. He wasn't the first choice of everybody and he still divides opinion today on his merits as a No 8. For me, he has always been a classic player of the game.

Nick Easter is not coming from left field to win his first England cap, he's coming from rugby's old school.

The first time I met him was when Easter moved to the Harlequins on loan. His arrival coincided with a kangaroo court session and the old hands in the changing room smelt fresh blood. Easter never flinched, he took all the abuse on offer, sank a few pints and then turned the tables and cranked up the pace.

It wasn't pretty but it signalled that Nick Easter had arrived and wouldn't back down. The new man had made his intentions clear. He is top dog at Harlequins. Player of the season every year, hard as nails, the biggest ball carrier, the new Keith Wood of the club.

This is not a strange England selection, as some have suggested, this is the epitome of picking on form. And it feeds into the philosophy of Phil Vickery, the captain who wants to build a band of brothers in the forward pack who are hard as nails and can start winning England their reputation back as having the nastiest, most bruising eight in international rugby.

I had the great fortune of taking the field with Easter and have seen at first hand what he can offer. First of all, he is one of the most hard-nosed competitors I have come across. Every time he takes the field it is with one purpose only, to dominate. He takes his rugby seriously, and perhaps the shock that has greeted his selection may point more to the fact that, just maybe, rugby didn't take him seriously.

His journey to the top has seen him hop from club to club in the lower, but well-respected, ranks of places such as Rosslyn Park and Orrell, before he got a shot at the Premiership. 'Have boots will travel' would pigeon-hole him nicely.

He has serious rugby experience, not all top flight but it doesn't matter. He has learnt to look after himself and every time he has stepped up a level he has delivered. From close to rucks, Easter drives into the big defenders with tremendous leg drive and generates momentum in places he has no right to. Out in the midfield, hanging off backs from off-the-top line-outs, he always gets over the gain line, and more often than not stays on his feet. This allows two things to happen that are key in international rugby. His team can either generate a strong driving maul, draining the lifeblood out of opposition forwards, or, as three defenders struggle to drag him down, the ball can be shifted away from the point of contact and sent in search of those vacant spaces.

The key to Easter is his ability to bowl a heavy ball – it is a cricketing term I have used before and it means that while many bowlers can send the ball down the wicket at the same pace, only a few can take the bat out of your hand. Easter is definitely in the rip-your-bat-out-of-your-hand category.

Luckily there is brain to go with the brawn, and he picks

tremendous lines off the fringes. Charging back against the direction of play, against the grain, is one of his favourite moves, attacking a tackler's weak inside shoulder. He is a line-out forward, almost a prerequisite nowadays, and has terrific hands.

So much for the good bits. As always, there are worries. His tackle technique could be adjusted down a foot as he has a tendency to go a little high, especially when compared to the man he is replacing, Joe Worsley, who rattles your ankles. Easter must also make sure he gets his hands dirtier at rucks. He has been picked at No 6, and blind-side flanker will mean a lot more work in the darkness than he is used to in his free-spirited role of No 8 at Quins.

The big question that remains is whether he can cut it in a white shirt. He has limited experience at the highest levels and the step up will be a shock. He will be coming in after a shining light of the season so far, Dan Ward-Smith of Bristol, popped a knee and expectations will be high.

Today will be a learning experience that should play to his strengths, and while England are in the mood to go back to basics Easter could prove to be a straight-A student.

The sweet pusher

Jason Robinson has a secret addiction and he has peddled his illicit substances to the England rugby team. I am not proud of the fact that I was one of his clients, lurking around outside his room, itching for my next hit and fidgeting until this most unlikely of pushers turned up.

Jason, you see, is the Mr Big of the chocolate world and he had a captive market when this sweetest form of indulgence was banned from the England team hotel at Pennyhill Park. So Stalinist was the clampdown that bellboys and hotel staff had been ordered not to make mercy missions to the corner shop, and such was the climate of fear that we dared not even look at a Crunchie in a provocative manner. But cometh the hour, cometh the man, and Jason would turn up with boxes of chocolate thanks to his sponsor Cadbury's.

He would walk the hotel corridors whispering 'cocoa, cocoa, who wants cocoa?', pressing packets of Buttons and bars of Dairy Milk through half-open doors and into sweaty palms. He just couldn't get enough of the stuff, and the only time I have seen him move quicker than on a rugby field was when the chocolate Rice Krispie cakes were brought out on the Friday before an international. Billy Whizz? He was like a puff of smoke, one minute standing next to me, the next half a building away, face and pockets filled with sticky treats, munching like a happy schoolboy.

It is this side to Jason that is most missed by the players at Sale and England – his generosity of time and spirit, his dry sense of humour that helped puncture stress, and his infectious enthusiasm and rock-solid professionalism. The World Cup final try, the Grand Final tries and the scorched earth campaign against Wales will live in our memories.

A lot of people have taken credit for pulling England through their 2003 World Cup quarter-final against Wales, but it was a piece of individual brilliance by Jason that turned the game upon its head. Gathering the ball up on the left-hand side of the pitch, miles from the Welsh tryline, he set off across the field in search of a gap. When there wasn't one, he did what he always did and created one.

A right-angled turn and a change of gear, acceleration like a sidewinder snake, a burst of power to shrug off the tackles, an outside arc to take the scrambling Welsh out of the equation and a pinpoint pass for the try. You can see what he's trying to do, but you just don't believe it is possible that someone can cram all of that skill into a split second of natural athleticism and instinct. I can honestly say that I was disappointed to score the try he made against Wales – Jason deserved to finish that off on his own.

However, for all his class on the international stage, I will remember Jason most for a training session years ago at Sandhurst. Jason was not in the England side, he was on the bench, and his team of replacements were running the ball at the starting XV for one of Phil Larder's defensive sessions. The ball was moved from side to side when a loose pass was thrown and Iain Balshaw intercepted. He was off, and when Iain Balshaw intercepts Iain Balshaw scores. The rest of us stood and watched the inevitable. But not Jason. Keen to impress he set off after Balshaw, like a cheetah hunting down a gazelle, the short powerful sprinter against the languid, graceful, suddenly terrified beast. For the first time, there was fear in Iain's eyes – he was thinking about the abuse he would cop, he was worried his gas would be deemed flat – and to counter it, he put his foot to the floor. It was to no avail. Jason had Balshaw's ankles in sight and 10 yards out the blond Lancastrian was grounded. Jason Robinson had arrived. He had let his feet do the talking and we had witnessed a truly remarkable piece of pace and desire. It is this killer combination that won him respect as a league player. League is one of the great sports, with physicality, intensity, skill, and courage, and I grew up idolising Jason as a rugby player. His precocious talent had him playing at the top level while still only a schoolboy. When he switched codes, he continued to possess that wow factor. His work ethic impressed us the most, and he wanted to prove he could kick, that he could ruck, that he could understand the weird nuances of rugby union. Jason takes nothing for granted. He is a most gracious, generous and mild-mannered superstar.

Jason Robinson is one of a kind, and I have the fillings to prove it.

Rock solid

Richard Hill is often called the best rugby player England ever produced. I was lucky to see his skill up close and know how valuable he was to his nation. But he never liked a fanfare when playing and it looked as if he was going to try and retire on the quiet.

Having failed by a whisker to make the Heineken Cup semi-final last Sunday, Richard Hill has played his last full game. He may appear for Saracens against Bristol on the final day of the season, but I hope it is nothing more than a trot-out because the well is empty, the knee is shot. The great man must not risk his health any more.

His going will mark the passing of an era. Teamed up with Neil Back and Lawrence Dallaglio, these boys took on the world. Hill was never as eye-catching as the other two – he never had Back's blond shock of hair or the muscular swagger of Dallaglio – but by God, was he effective. Without him, England were unbalanced. With him, we won the World Cup.

My favourite memory of Hill does not come in a match. It took place well before the kick-off when he, Back and Dallaglio would head out on to the field together and do a lap of the pitch. The three of them were like wild animals on the prowl. Cold, calculating. Their eyes shifting, watching, listening, waiting for their moment. Powerful, athletic, ruthless.

I would always go out ahead of them, not to warm up, but to watch as they roamed and threatened. For a back it was like having your very own pack of hunting dogs.

To see them trot around so gracefully, and yet so purposefully, was a great joy. It gave you confidence, it set you up. You knew what they were about to do, what they would put themselves through for the team. Their levels of commitment, bravery and street smarts were beyond those of ordinary athletes. I half expected them to pee on the corner flags, marking their territory.

They were a special unit and Hill was arguably the key component. At his peak, between 1999 and 2003, his was the first name down on a world XV team-sheet. People talk about what made him special and they say it was the unseen work. For me, what set him apart was his ability to be in the right place at the right time.

In defence and attack he was sheer class. Simply put, he just understood rugby. Goal-scorers and try-scorers have to be in the right place to finish off moves, but equally you need a guy who is in the right place to turn over the opposition with his technique in the tackle. You need someone who can win matches with his technique at the breakdown, and who has a built-in tracking system for the ball.

Hill knew instinctively where the danger would come from – he could see the game two rucks ahead and was there waiting when the opposition's thrust arrived, ready to snuff it out and, if possible, launch you up to the other end of the field.

In his early days he was a good ball carrier, quick, dynamic, power-ful and with an incredible engine. He would look after you as a back and, when all options seemed dead, he would get with you and protect you. He was a good line-out player, with great hands.

He was a tough man, and would stand toe-to-toe with anyone, but he wasn't interested in fighting. He played hard and he played fair. He was a true player's player. His value to the England squad could be seen when he pulled a hamstring during the opening game of the World Cup in 2003.

England had a belting squad. Players like Graham Rowntree, Simon Shaw and Austin Healey missed out on initial selection, so if there was a danger you would be out injured for some time, then you were packed off home pretty quickly, no carrying of dead weight.

There was never a thought of sticking Hilly on a plane. Never a thought of replacing him with some able-bodied young tyro to make sure we had the numbers for training. No, it was simply a case of, 'Richard, when you're ready, let us know and you're straight back in.'

And when he did come back, he did the business as if he had never been away. His focus was always pin-point. He was not a nightclubber unless the job was done, and even then he was bloody useless. For a man with so much rhythm and grace on a rugby field, his dancing, singing, and drinking had very little style or substance.

He loved going to zoos and drinking coffee on his day off. He was always quiet, measured and assured, and was never given to great words before matches or in team meetings. He just got things done. He loved his massages, he loved his computer. He laughed, but didn't tell jokes. No ego, no big emotion, no neon lights, no daft haircut, just the kid next door who was a bloody genius of a rugby player.

Injuries robbed Hill of some years late in his career, though by then he had achieved it all as an England player. At club level his loyalty has been rock solid. He may regret a lack of club trophies, but stability, honesty, loyalty meant more to him when the big clubs came knocking. I doubt we will see a very different Richard Hill on his last day as a player. No trophy, no big final, no play-offs. A sheepish smile, a wave to friends, a hug for his team-mates, is about all we'll get. He doesn't want trumpets and fanfares, he never has and he never will. That's your job. If you are going to the game, make sure you don't let Hill hobble off into retirement quite so easily. Make sure the quiet man is embarrassed by the din of appreciation. He must be made to listen, to understand the profound effect he has had on English rugby, its supporters and his team-mates.

Just don't expect him to enjoy it.

Dallaglio demands respect

Lawrence Dallaglio was a force of nature on the rugby field. He was a supremely talented athlete but what set him apart was his hard-nosed will to win. This is what saw him come back from a career-ending injury and meant England lost a large chunk of their invincibility when he retired.

I am claustrophobic, so I hated the pile-ups in the playground. I hated caving in the Lake District with my school, and I hate it when a pack of forwards lands on my head. That feeling of being trapped, of having the breath squeezed out of you, of the walls closing in. So, you can imagine my joy when, after a heavy fall against Doncaster, I found myself having a scan. For those of you not acquainted with this wonder of modern technology, they lay you flat in a tube the size of a small post box, hand you a panic button and go for a cup of tea while pneumatic drill noises go off in your ears.

Ah, the joys of being a professional athlete. My shoulders were playing up again – even after four operations they wouldn't give me a break. As I lay there, staring at the roof of the scanner less than two inches from my massive konk, I couldn't help wonder why we do it. Or how sportspeople manage to stay so positive and upbeat about the painful and lengthy rehabilitation process that will surely follow any serious injury.

Jonny Wilkinson has had nigh on two years off the field with everything from stingers to a dodgy appendix. He came back all smiles, setting what must be a record for even his Herculean powers of positivity.

Richard Hill spent eight months fixing his knee, only for it to go again in the first 20 minutes of the first Lions Test. There are many more, but Lawrence Bruno Nero Dallaglio probably eclipsed them all. Four months after rearranging his lower right leg in ways a contortionist would struggle to comprehend he took the field against Cardiff. Written off in some quarters, he was back. And worryingly for his opponents, he was hungry, he wanted respect and his England place back.

When I heard he was fit for the game, I could only imagine the number of expletives that were muttered in South Wales. A few mouths would have needed washing out in the England squad room as well. Maybe I am different – I doubt it – but when I used to weigh up my chances of getting into the England squad I never factored in people who had retired 13 months earlier.

For me, I was over the moon when Will Carling, Phil de Glanville and Jeremy Guscott headed off for pastures new. To be honest – and call me overly ambitious – while I was wishing them a happy retirement and talking sweet pleasantries about the marvellous careers they had enjoyed, I was secretly wishing they had retired years earlier. As far as I saw it, they were in my way. It won't even have crossed Dallaglio's mind that he might have been blocking some youngster's rise up the rankings. And why should it?

He reckoned he had a lot to offer and much to set right before heading off into the sunset. First and foremost, he wanted Wasps to get the respect he feels they deserved. In much the same way that his football team, Chelsea, have felt the respect they are due is not forthcoming, Dallaglio believed that Leicester got all the superlatives while Wasps were overlooked. He wanted Wasps to be remembered as the best team of his generation and to go beyond Leicester's record of four league titles and two European cups.

He was livid when all the talk ahead of 2005's Zurich final revolved around the grand farewells of Neil Back and Martin Johnson, and not about the skill and determination his team had been showing. He has always been uncompromising and his drive has always been to win – whether it's rugby or taking golf lessons on the sly to win big-money games on tour.

In the pre-match changing room it's like having an East End gangster in there with you. I've played with him all the way through from the England Under-21s and he still scares me. His worth to England was no more evident than on that fateful night in Sydney. With Johnson staring down on us, Dallaglio prowled up and down the changing room, quite literally driving players into a frenzy of anticipation.

Self-belief is a valuable commodity in international rugby and Dallaglio, with his Italian connections, was never going to be short of confidence. Some people call it arrogance; I call it knowing that you can make a difference. That's what drives him forward, that's what helps him bounce back from injury. And in the suffocating world of international rugby, it can be the difference between winning and losing.

A legend of the game

Lawrence Dallaglio does not do half measures. His career has had its blips – some self-inflicted, others not – but at no time did you ever imagine that he would not bounce back. Lol is a man who always gave the impression that he was going to squeeze every last drop from life.

People talk of his emotional intensity, and it is what makes him such a powerful figure on and off the field. This is not a man who will sit back and let things just happen – he will dictate the terms and life will just have to deal with the consequences. People listen when he speaks because they see what he gives to the cause, be it club or country. Before the 2003 World Cup he helped set the tone among the older players, showing the younger ones what was needed. He would lift weights during extra training sessions under the stands at Twickenham, pushing himself to the brink of collapse, eyes burning, body glistening with sweat, pain etched on his face.

You did not get respect from him, you earned it. He was from the old school, he earned his stripes in the Will Carling era. Reputations counted for nothing, and if you came up short you were reminded of your weakness in the most brutal fashion.

From the very first moment I toured with Lawrence in 1993, I knew I was in the presence of someone different. Even as a 21-year-old he had an aura. It saw him winning the Sevens World Cup in 1993 and touring with England in 1994. It meant that when he was faced by players like Zinzan Brooke, Toutai Kefu and Andre Venter, he always fancied his chances.

He was not one to shy away from a challenge and his pre-match talk was so East End gangsteresque that he could easily take over from Vinnie Jones as Hollywood's favourite British hard man. Five minutes before a Test, jaw out, finger pointing, tear in the eye – you bloody listened to Lawrence no matter what he had to say.

I only ever saw him lost for words once. We were injured on the 2001 Lions tour and were doing ambassador duty at the governor of Australia's residence. Twenty minutes in, we were approached by a gentleman who told Lawrence that he was one of his heroes.

'I don't think I have ever seen a finer rugby player and man,' he added. Lawrence, who pretended to blush, said thanks, and asked if there was anything he could do in return. 'An autograph would be fantastic,' the gentleman said, 'because when my children find out that I have met the great Martin Johnson they will be so jealous.'

It is hard to believe that would happen today, because Lawrence has developed beyond a rugby player and into a brand. He is so many things to so many people and they all form the fabric that makes him the man he is.

Dedicated family man, friend, businessman, charmer. He always knows the best place in town, he understands the chat, and he gets you places you thought were reserved for pop moguls.

There is some bad stuff. I never thought he could pass a rugby ball that well; that side of his game was clumsy and manufactured in his early days. He definitely can't kick a ball. But that is about it.

Incredible pace, tremendous ball-carrying ability, unbelievable at the breakdown. He knows when to accept the yellow card, he knows when his team need it. What is more important is his ability to kill the game. An all-enveloping tackle was his favoured modus operandi. While others would go low, Lawrence just turned the lights out.

He has been kicked, punched and smashed, and never once has he questioned his style of play or the smarts of what he was doing. In fact, the more players go after him, the better he feels – he takes it as a compliment. No matter what others did, no matter what happened off the field, he never faltered in his belief of his club or country, and he maintained an unwavering faith that both teams would succeed.

Lawrence Dallaglio was a true rugby original who managed to get the very best out of himself and those around him. Very few of us can say that.

The real deal

In 2009 Dan Carter signed for Perpignan in a record deal. A lot of people questioned the value of him as a player. But you only have to see the immediate impact he had in France that year and then later the shock of his injury in the 2011 World Cup to see that his worth goes beyond cold cash.

The club shop at Perpignan is a shrine to the city's favourite new son, Dan Carter. It could not have more paraphernalia if it tried. Watches with Carter as a logo instead of the famous Cartier. T-shirts, jerseys, even a range of underpants. I have a signed pair of pants that will be worth more than gold in the South West of France should the new man manage to bring home the club championship. It has not been seen in Perpignan for more than 50 years.

Carter has six months to deliver. When I was there, the crowd were salivating at the prospect of being entertained by their new toy. The president has delivered them the world's best rugby player, and they have great expectations.

Being successful is no small task for a man who has only ever really known two teams, and neither have had much French chit-chat in among the banter. You have to wonder, in a 15-man game, how one man with no knowledge of the local area, players, or coaching staff agreed to such a mission impossible.

Money was obviously a motivating factor, and at some £35,000 a game, it would have been very difficult to turn down. But the risks are very high.

Before last week's Heineken Cup game against Leicester, Carter looked nervous, something he admitted in post-match interviews. You can understand why.

The Perpignan stadium is as close to the Colosseum as you will find. The pitch a good 10 feet below the lowest level of seating, making it seem that there is no escape for visiting teams once their giant pack has you begging for mercy. It holds only 15,000 but hours before kick-off you know the intensity of support will be magnificent.

They are tough, and love their rugby. The former England winger Dan Luger played there for a season. On his first day in Perpignan one of his huge forwards brought a dead sheep into the changing room, hacked off a leg and gave it to him as a gift. That is hard core even by All Black standards.

Carter reacted as he does best. He did not get drawn into the circus, and he did not respond with Harlem Globetrotter rugby. He knows that is the fastest way to undo his reputation.

When the game against Leicester started his tackling was solid, his distribution never hurried. True, he dropped a couple of balls, missed a couple of kicks, got speared by Harry Ellis, but it was enough to pick up the man of the match award. The Perpignan crowd were satisfied – Carter was having an immediate impact.

What is interesting is that he could have had an effect if he had been sitting in the stands. Call it a placebo effect, just remember that Carter is no faux fix, no sugared pill. He is the real deal and is one of those few players, no matter in which sport, who can revitalise a club before they have kicked a ball, swung a racket, or rowed a stroke.

It has taken them years of dedicated hard work and commitment to their trade to get themselves into such a position, and it is why they command the big bucks. Some coaches will negate this effect. Instead they will point to hard work and commitment, telling us there is no magic wand.

Maybe. But if this is the case, then how did England get to the final of the 2007 World Cup? They did it because Jonny Wilkinson was back in the side. At one point they were on the brink of going out in the group stage yet just a month later fighting for the right to retain the Webb Ellis Cup.

He was not at the top of his game, but he has a presence, that galvanises those around him and fills them with confidence. Players want to perform better when people like Jonny and Dan Carter are around.

Off the field there are coaches such as Warren Gatland and Shaun Edwards who have a similar vibe. They build up an aura by being in total control of their surroundings and environment.

Carter knows that for Perpignan to win anything this season he will have to do more than just turn up. Yet having him in the team has given Perpignan a 10-point advantage before the game has kicked off.

A whole town has been given a shot of Carter confidence. It does not come cheap, but it might just prove to be money well spent.

England's most famous rugby player

Jonny Wilkinson is the golden boy of English rugby. I saw him change from a young hopeful to the country's shyest pin-up and first millionaire player. And while his training and commitment made him special, it was also putting his playing career at risk. But when I met up with him in London after England had lost the 2007 World Cup final, changes were starting to take place.

I have to pick Jonny Wilkinson up from his hotel but cannot find him anywhere. How hard can it be to spot England's most famous rugby player in a breakfast room? I scan the room five times before I notice him, and then I understand why he disappeared so perfectly. It is his hair.

Gone is the precision cut, and in its place is a very dubious mullet. Sitting in a corner with hair long at the back and longer on top, he looks like an unkempt woman. The man, who is famous for his neurotic workaholic rugby life, has gone all boho.

We say our hellos and head to the car. He tells me he has just come back from a pre-season tour with Newcastle, even though injury meant he was unable actually to play. He will be ready for the opening fixture in 10 days and has spent much of the summer recovering from a shoulder operation and working out how to tell if his damn-near-perfect physique is about to break down again. Jonny explains that it is all about finding more balance, about trying to get a grip.

'I've almost got little alarm bells on different parts of my body that go off when I train too much. It's almost ridiculous how quickly they just kick in now.' Part of his problem in the early years was that he did not realise quite how hard he was pushing himself.

'Because I was in the early stages of creating an attrition effect on everything, it took a while, and then I got to the stage where they had all worn down. Then all the injuries came at once. Now if I go too far or too hard, I get reminded of it the next day by the fact that I might just have no legs, or I might wake up and I am struggling with something.'

He says he is learning how to cope with this new system, but that it is also giving him the motivation to expand his playing career and capabilities. This is a theme that has been evident throughout Jonny's career.

When many people were happy to call it a day, he was always striving for perfection, looking to find out what was inside him, how much better he could become. It was inspiring to watch, and set the tone for any team he was part of, but you could not help wondering if he was paying a high price for all that dedication. At times he seemed to have the weight of the world on his shoulders.

He still talks of the unknown factors, the things outside his control, which were killing him. 'The unknown is the pressure, what the results would mean, the selections. Those things would be negatives to me – I've turned them around and they have become positives,' he says.

Today, Jonny says that rather than imprisoning him, those unknowns are liberating, and when he runs out on to the training field it is with a smile and a renewed sense of anticipation.

That he enjoys what he does becomes very clear when we head to Twickenham to coach a group of Rosslyn Park kids on their kicking technique. Faced with a gaggle of excited boys and girls, and their often even more giddy parents, Jonny goes to work. The smile is broad, the questions genuine and the plaudits true. Never a wince or a moan when asked for an autograph or photo, just a gentleman personified.

But even here, on a day off, when he could let things slide, there are signs of what make him unique. Each kid is given full concentration. When he is showing how to perform a task, not one kick is sliced or misplaced. Every conversion cuts through the centre of the posts, and every time a kid puts a ball on the kicking tee, Jonny cannot resist tinkering and adjusting its position so that it's absolutely perfect.

Compulsive behaviour, genius or lunacy? Time runs on, the parents are getting restless, but Jonny will not let a player finish with a bad kick. He sends everyone home knowing that the last kick they took at Twickenham was a great one. The only way he likes it.

You get the feeling with Jonny that he likes to have order in all parts of his life, and that he plays his best rugby when the structure of the team is set up to provide him with that. The changes to England's management may well help him rediscover his best form, and he has reacted positively to the introduction of Martin Johnson at the top of the tree.

'The first week with Johnno was a good week. We were re-introduced into a lifestyle that supports your rugby and integrates with it to make it better.'

Jonny speaks about a code of ethics, conduct and lifestyle, of a style of behaviour both on and off the field that creates momentum, gives a team a 16th player and a shot to win every match, no matter who it is against. Talk to him about what he would like to change in himself and Jonny mentions the confidence of his young challenger, Danny Cipriani. Skills count only for so much, the rest is down to having the guts to back your vision, of telling the team how you want it done and dictating the terms of engagement.

'I look back at myself at [Cipriani's] age, and that was the thing I always found hardest. Maybe it was because I was surrounded by such high-profile players that I had grown up with. I thought, "who was I to tell these guys what to do?" I didn't even have my own vision of the game, I was just happy to fit into what anyone told me should be done. It took me a while, as the game went professional, to get a grip on what I truly believed in, what made me different to someone else.'

He says that is the reason he has stayed at Newcastle, because he has a chance to play a central role in moving the club forward. For other players the time was right to move, for him it was right to stay put and help drive things forward, to try to put into place the vision that he has for the game and the team. You also get the feeling that he likes the familiar surroundings, and that they will let him relax even more.

A keen guitar player, he has formed a band with his brother on drums, Carl Hayman, the giant Kiwi prop, on rhythm guitar, and the Falcons kit man on vocals. The noise must be quite something. A few years ago the thought of Jonny in a band would have made me giggle. Today I am pleased he is having a laugh and messing about with his mates.

At the end of our day together, as he heads off with a kit bag in one hand and a guitar over his shoulder, I am struck by how happy and relaxed he seems, and for the first time in years I do not feel worried for Jonny.

A man who doesn't do things by halves

The text message hit my phone at six in the morning. 'Meet me at the gym, the hotel will give you directions'.

It was like a John le Carré novel. The man who craves secrecy was giving me an audience. The hunt for Jonny Wilkinson was on.

It was a journey that would take me through the South of France, in and out of two different airports and three different stadiums to the east and west of Toulon, and a wrong turn into a naval base.

When I found England's missing man, he was on a basketball court, taking part in a game that looked like a rugby all-stars match.

Flinging the ball about were Pierre Mignoni, Juan Martín Fernández Lobbe, and Joe van Niekerk. Felipe Contepomi was watching. Wilkinson was in among them, smile on his face, back where he belonged.

After years of injuries and a seemingly endless spiral of negative rugby moments, Wilkinson left Newcastle for a new life in Toulon. There is no doubt that it is suiting him.

He is playing well, kicking his goals, though not all of them, standing flat, asking questions of defences. His distribution is great, his kicking out of hand is aggressive from penalties, and his short kicking game is improving. He is still very sharp at getting counter-punches on the scoreboard, drop goals and penalties keeping the team ticking over.

Wilkinson is standing on the cusp of a comeback that could rank up there with the best of them. But looking at his tanned face, it brought back an image that I could not shake. The ghost of his past kept leering out at me like a sun-stripped memento mori.

This is not a man who does things by halves. He is all or nothing, and it has cost him dear. His disregard for his own safety on the field has been his biggest weakness.

Just like the friend who drinks and smokes too much, you fear that one day the hard living will catch up with him. Injured in the dying seconds against Saracens a month ago, the game won, you wanted him to stay down. He got up, and 30 seconds later he was smashing into someone else.

As we walk away from the basketball court, and head for the harbour of Toulon, the sunlight and million-euro boats half answering my questions about why he made the move, I ask why he does it?

'My soul would eke away if I was being hidden in the defensive line. If I lose the intention of trying to do something better for the team, then my soul will go.'

But what about your importance to the team? 'No. Once I am involved, I am involved properly. What you do daily and how you behave is how you will play. Corners you cut in your prep, lifestyle, and decision-making will appear on the field.'

I cannot help but smile, remembering that this is a man whose training often resembles a battle with obsessive-compulsive disorder. I ask if he is still training to extremes. His answers tell me that he is still doing too much, and making excuses for it. The oft-used phrases come out, 'I have not played in 10 months . . . need to give myself a foundation . . . a bank account of training from which you can pluck.'

But there is also a realisation that he cannot internalise too many of the pressures. 'I have moved into the middle ground, away from a person trying to cover every base and trying to have the game done before I go on to the field. I now try to be someone longing for the unknown. Before, I feared the unknown a little bit.'

Now he does the preparation so that he can throw off the shackles when he is playing. He wants to be ready, physically and mentally, to take opportunities as they present themselves. This is true for his life on and off the field.

For the Wilkinson of today, the 'unknown is what makes life brilliant.' He says he never lost his passion for the game, it is just that during the dark times it turned into something different. Limited by injuries, the passion morphed into a fight for survival. 'When you are injured, all doors close and you are grabbing and clutching at whatever you can . . . Here, it is about playing for me.'

It was not easy to turn his back on Newcastle, especially when he wanted to leave it a better place than when he arrived. But by the end he felt he was taking more than he was giving back.

I ask him if the money was a factor in his leaving the North East after so many years. 'It's a professional world, but the money doesn't last. All I am interested in is going out there and seeing what I can achieve. That fulfils me. Money has never done that.'

I remind myself that this is the man who turned down £1 million to pose for *Hello!* magazine. 'If it all finishes tomorrow you can say, fine, that was good enough, because right then that was all I had anyway. Money can't buy that.' It is a point he returns to at different times during our day together.

I ask him if England are good enough to win the autumn internationals, and if Twickenham can become a fortress like it was in the days when he was in his pomp. 'You go in with that attitude, I have never considered going into a game with anything less. What England fans can expect is England to keep getting better and better and better.'

I ask him about the world leaders in his position, men like Matt Giteau and Dan Carter. 'They are ultra professional, like brilliant rugby-playing machines. They come in and the team functions around them and they don't try too hard. They make the right decisions over 80 minutes and that is what I am learning to do again.'

And it is a learning experience for Wilkinson today. No matter what he has done in the past, the clocks have been reset. He is earning his stripes all over again. His game is not yet at the heights he used to be able to reach. He is not error-free and there is the occasional wild pass, but he is less robotic.

As we swap the holiday glamour of the quayside for a secret walking route that he loves to take when seeking solitude, I ask if it is a conscious decision to rely more on his instincts.

Is he finally giving in to his animal side, a mountain goat rather than man-machine? He ponders this, then decides that he is a 'robotic goat'. Well, it's a start, I suppose. 'Rugby will never change for me. It's not about anything else other than sharing experiences with people around you.' This is an important point for him because he still hankers after anonymity.

When I ask another Toulon player, he admits he does not know where Wilkinson lives. It is almost as if he has a split personality, keeping people at a friendly arm's length. And if I want reminding of the balancing act that being Wilkinson requires, I am given it as we say our goodbyes.

At the end of our walk through the hills, he has to negotiate his car down a ludicrously steep slope. He cuts the corner too tight, and gets the front jammed. His back right tyre is on the edge of a rocky ridge. The left wheel is three feet off the ground. This is not good, he is having an *Italian Job* moment.

I tell him to get out of the car before hopes of an England revival tumble to the bottom of a French gorge. He gets out of the car, his face drained of its colour. The last time I saw it so pale was years ago when he went down with a first bout of shoulder trouble. And this is the problem you have with him.

He does everything right, and is the most professional of professionals. Yet he is still the master of putting himself in harm's way. And it happens so fast, that there is nothing you can do except sit and pray he gets away with it.

An inspirational crackpot who lived for the game

I've always thought of Jonny Wilkinson as a crackpot. I still do and it's the way he goes about things that sets him out of the ordinary. The lad was born with talent, and there can be no doubt about the gifts he was given. But that is only part of the story. His brilliance was achieved through his dedication to his craft.

He worked harder than anyone to maximise his talent, even to the point that his own physical and mental well-being came into question. When the rest of England's players were already deep in their baths, Dave Alred, the kicking coach, would drive his car onto the pitch so that Jonny could keep practising in the beams of his headlights. In terms of running he would do the drills and switch off his brain to pain.

When others were limping off after heavy contact sessions he was just getting warmed up. No matter how long a session was he would do each drill as if it was the only one, holding nothing back, giving his all each and every time. I still don't know how do you do that.

His actions off the field, just as much as his points scoring on it, had a profound effect on the people around him. You were amazed and felt a little frightened by his focus but damned if you didn't want to try and do better at the same time.

And just as he lifted you by his actions he also tried hard to make you see the game his way. In the England camp he would always give a presentation on the Friday before the final team run. It was fascinating to see the way his brain worked in coloured markers and flip charts. The pitch drawn perfectly and symmetrically to scale, his handwriting any teacher would die for. His talks were always 15 minutes long and by the time they were over the whole team knew exactly what was happening on any given area of the field at any given time.

I may not have agreed with him on all of it, but I certainly understood what was needed. And no matter what I may have thought tactically he would usually do something remarkable and shoot my arguments down by his sheer will to succeed. People will always talk about the World Cup but in my view the best example of Jonny's skills was in the Grand Slam decider in March 2003. He was fly-half perfection. He made plus 20 tackles, covered the field like a flanker, nailed his penalties and conversions like a marksman, was inch perfect with his kicks from hand and dropped goals, off each foot into and against the wind.

But with Jonny, the playing part of the game was only part of the puzzle. He really was the first proper rugby heart-throb of the professional era and it didn't always sit easily. His drive for success on the field and hunt for perfection was called obsessive behaviour off it; his ability to command and direct the show during the game sometimes meant he felt a little helpless outside of it; and his role as leading man and fancy dan was a difficult fit for someone who loves their privacy. Ironically, as he has found more happiness and balance off the field so his game at the highest level has creaked. But if I am honest, who could begrudge him that and when I have seen him in his new setting of the South of France he seems a much happier person.

I have two memories that should tell you everything that matters about Jonny. When that final whistle went after that drop goal in 2003 I found myself jumping up and down with the man who would become a national icon. At that moment you see two mates just jumping up and down like overgrown kids. It is the pure joy of sport and friendship and it is Jonny at his best. There is no guard or fear, you just see someone happy because they did what they could and they delivered for their team when it mattered.

The second memory comes courtesy of my wife who was in hospital during the World Cup when we had come close to losing our now seven-year-old son Archie. The midwives would run through and ask if he had texted, and always the thoughtful fella, he stayed in touch during that difficult time. The midwives would look horrified when Caro told them she had deleted the texts – they could not understand how you could delete a text from Jonny. But what matters is he sent them.

So when people ask why Jonny mattered as a rugby player the answer is simple – he was someone who lived for the game and his team-mates and made us all better through his actions on and off the field.

Brian O'Driscoll: warrior, believer and ultimately, winner

Some men define their country's style of rugby. Martin Johnson has his unapologetic English obstinacy. For French flair how about Philipe Sella or Serge Blanco. Wales had Jonathan Davies, Scotland Finlay Calder.

In the southern hemisphere, you say Sean Fitzpatrick, Ruben Kruger and Tim Horan and you know exactly what you will get. But for Ireland, it was always a little harder to get it spot on. Don't get me wrong, they had some great players, just not one of whom you could say conclusively 'that's Irish rugby, that's what it's all about'.

Men such as Keith Wood had that hard edge when wearing the Lions jersey, an intense presence that never let up. In the backs, the great Brendan Mullin showed the lovely flat-out balance that will stand any test of time. But no one combined it all to showcase the full-on, ferocious beauty that Irish rugby can achieve.

Well, no one until Brian O'Driscoll. After a decade of trying, he finally brought home the silverware, and with it came as close as anyone ever has of becoming the quintessential Irish player. The big play, the big tackle, a team in need, he delivered until his head was knocked so hard in that brutal second Lions Test in 2009 that he could hardly keep his feet.

The dream of a perfect year may have gone with his concussion, yet there was plenty to be proud of. The Grand Slam he led Ireland to was a masterpiece of experience and youth from Declan Kidney and his evergreen captain. They toughed out games when they had to and turned screws when opportunities arose.

Come the autumn their self-belief snatched a draw against Australia and then they delivered in another humdinger against South Africa. As if that was not enough, the Heineken Cup went to Leinster as the second team of Irish provincial rugby finally managed to get the Munster monkey off their backs.

In the middle of it all was O'Driscoll, warrior, believer and, ultimately, winner. He tops the stats on dropped goals, tries, outside breaks, inside breaks, tackles and turnovers. He often plays like a flanker, forgetting that a back should be a long way from the bump and grind of the pack. He has redefined a midfield man's priorities.

However, for all his skills and fearlessness he is not the perfect player. Much like Irish rugby itself he has weaknesses that can let him down at the most crucial moments.

His kicking game is patchy and he can overplay his hand, forcing things too much so that he ends up putting the ball on the floor more often than a less-talented player would deem acceptable. But, for me at least, the blips are what make him all the more outstanding. Working out your weaknesses and developing a game plan that allows you to ignore them is the real mark of genius. To be brought down by our shortcomings is par for the course, to make them irrelevant is something else altogether.

I do not collect rugby shirts as a habit, but my signed original match shirt of O'Driscoll is going nowhere. I was lucky to see the man close-up, and there are memories that will never fade. For a start he was one of the untidiest room-mates I ever had. My anally retentive side of the room was nicely packed away and tidy, his side looked as if it had been hit by a bomb.

He is one of the pastiest people I have ever seen. White does not do him justice. He is more of a pale blue. He used to look like a geography teacher when wearing glasses, and his middle name is Gerald.

However, in 2001 on the Lions tour, Austin Healey put on some boxing gloves the fitness adviser had brought along and started sparring with O'Driscoll. Brian found this annoying and clipped him four times. Austin never saw them coming and we had to throw napkins in to stop the fight.

O'Driscoll's acceleration is astonishing. His try at the Gabba in the first Lions Test of 2001 was two breaks, a step, a standing start and still with the pace to get away. His hat-trick in Paris, when we wore the old-style shirts that weighed a tonne, still saw him run away from everyone with ease.

He is not afraid of a drink, but is a born ambassador. In his old house, he had a normal toilet and a urinal. Who has a urinal? There are songs – 'Waltzing O'Driscoll' – named after him. And he can come up with lines like this: 'Knowledge is knowing a tomato is a fruit; wisdom is knowing not to put it into a fruit salad.'

A complex and interesting character, O'Driscoll is acknowledged by some as the best Ireland has ever produced.

Ireland's best ever player

Brian O'Driscoll makes players do things they don't want to do. He sucks the air from around you like one of Voldemort's death-eaters. Confusion reigns for this king of pain.

I used to get different levels of adrenalin before matches; relaxed, excited, nervous, and the final, nerve jangling, please don't let me look an idiot. The last one I only ever really got against BOD. He always has a level of intensity, no matter if it is Leinster or Ireland, which is terrifying. He has a look that shows he wants to rip your head off. And trust me, for a self-acknowledged coward, there is nothing scarier than some psychotic pasty Irishman setting his sights on you.

Even when I am not playing, he can haunt my thoughts. Ten minutes after a Heineken Cup semi-final in 2011, I was in a TV studio when our host, Simon Lazenby, nonchalantly throws out the line that 'Brian O'Driscoll is the greatest rugby player Ireland have ever produced'. Sean Fitzpatrick, All Black legend; Paul Wallace, Lions winner; and me, Rodney Trotter lookalike, really jumped down his throat.

The off-the-cuff remarks often provide the greatest debates. 'Alex Ferguson is the greatest manager of all time'; 'Seve Ballesteros was the greatest thing to happen to European golf'; 'Daley Thompson is Britain's greatest athlete'. Suddenly everyone is an expert and they scream back at you that Alf Ramsey won a World Cup and Bill Shankly built Liverpool; that Tony Jacklin won in America first and Nick Faldo won more majors than anyone else this side of the Pond; that Linford Christie beat the Yanks and Roger Bannister ran the mile in sub four minutes.

It's all a matter of opinion. So, I threw three names straight back at the slightly stunned TV anchor; BOD? What about Mike Gibson, Willie John McBride and Fergus Slattery? The names sprung from my lips without a millisecond of thought – you can't allow an anchor to turn these men into also-rans without an argument.

But as easy as it was to defend them, it also got me thinking. I love a list. It's just that the more I kept mulling it over the more I kept coming back to O'Driscoll.

I never saw Willie John play apart from in old Lions footage. Mike Gibson has my father talking in hushed tones about his skills. As a child I remember Fergus, the wild crazy man, hunting down Englishmen. I threw those names back at Lazenby out of instinct rather than a close up, intimate knowledge of their abilities as rugby players.

O'Driscoll, however, I have seen up close. I have felt the full force of his power, seen the sheer acceleration as it happens a yard from me, and seen his eyes, nose to nose, when they are ready for battle.

Over the past 20 years, I have been lucky to go up against, watch or play with some special men. Horan was special, Bunce magnificent, Guscott magical, Tana the leader, Mortlock so brave, Gibbs immense, Jauzion so graceful, Bateman so underrated.

At international level I missed out on Sella, but saw him at club games. I played a charity match against Danie Gerber. Of the current crowd, Jaque Fourie is a match winner at the highest level, while Tindall will always be my go-to man in the afterlife because he stood with me in 2003. Sonny Bill scares me. But, no matter what I do, I still keep trying to find the best of the best and I still keep coming back to O'Driscoll.

I can never get away from his rawness. In terms of emotion, strength and speed. I now feel silly for throwing names back at Lazenby. How can I doubt O'Driscoll's greatness on the say-so of my old man, and the evidence of a few videos, stories and hazy memories? I must go on what I have witnessed and the simple, unarguable fact that when it matters, Brian delivers. That has to be the mark of greatness (my greatest regret in rugby will always be tearing my ankle ligaments the week before the first Lions Test in 2001, and being forced to watch BOD score that try from the stands at the Gabba, rather than alongside him).

No matter what state he finds himself in, he also always finds the answers. The hit he made on Danie Rossouw in the second Test in South Africa in 2009 was bigger than the Gibbs effort on Du Randt in 1997. The Ox was exhausted in 1997 when Gibbsy came steaming through the middle. Rossouw had just entered the field and is a known enforcer from the back row and was on his home ground. O'Driscoll dispatched him whence forth he came. Brian also crippled himself, but there was never a thought of self-preservation.

He leads, I am told, with inspirational words, and more importantly with inspirational deeds. A hat-trick in Paris as a kid makes him immortal in my eyes. Even after all these years, the hunger burns bright.

When he is challenged he responds. Whether it is the bloodless beating he dished out to Austin Healey in a Manly hotel lobby in 2001, or in a semi-final against Toulouse three weeks ago when he tried to apologise to team-mates for a yellow card and scored the winning try that wiped his slate clean. He is not afraid to speak his mind and was happy to be rude about England after beating us in 2004.

I have not forgotten his post-match speech when he spoke of 'so called world champions in a so-called fortress'. Yet he deals with his own great injustice with ambassadorial elegance. When Umaga and Mealamu did a job on him, even if they didn't want to hurt him, they wanted to send a message. Why? Because in 2005 when very few had the guts to question New Zealand's supremacy, O'Driscoll was open about his belief they were beatable. That's just the kind of player he is.

He has weaknesses, he makes errors. Technically you could pick him up on the left-hand pass or the overuse of the boot. In the end, though, the negatives are meaningless because he carries the true mark of greatness, and that is his ability to change a game at the highest level. A few people can do it on the odd occasion; to manage it over the span of a decade is nothing short of miraculous.

And for that fact alone, no matter how many names will be hurled at me, I am happy to say that this lad from Dublin is Ireland's best ever player.

An unquenchable fire

I was in the changing room at Twickenham when I heard that Mike Catt was retiring. There was no better place to be. I had the place to myself. It was eerily quiet. The Victorian baths stood empty, the walls had been given a lick of paint, the door was no longer where it used to be. Physically it had changed and spiritually it now belongs to another team.

But if I closed my eyes and drank in the silence, I could see my old friend standing there. Mike Catt was always there, the fire burning in his eyes.

That was what I first noticed about him. It was the kind of fire that differentiates the warrior king from the talented athlete, the great achiever from the nearly man.

Actually that's not quite true. What I really noticed first about Cattman was his clothes. They were rubbish. I was no model, but even I could tell that this guy had no idea about fashion.

Here was a young man new in the UK and it was as if he had spent the past few years on the moon rather than in South Africa. Denim, lumberjack shirts, and white socks. Not a good mix even in the Eighties, and fashion then was as bad as it got.

Still, you forgot all about that when he started to play. Flat on the line, flinging passes off both hands, ahead of his time, leaving his peers behind in terms of vision and guts. No matter the numbers in the stand, the enormity of the match, I simply had to shout 'Cattman' and the ball would fizz through the air. He could pick up a vibe, an intuition better than anyone.

We won some great matches, and we lost some even bigger

games together, none more so than Dublin 2001. A Grand Slam denied, it only fuelled him further.

England needed men like Mike Catt in those tough days, someone to pick you up by the bootstraps, to smile a cheeky smile, to get you back on the training paddock.

His skill and drive were a constant reminder that if you stuck to your guns, kept believing in what you were doing, then special things could happen. Nothing fazes him. This is a man who has been lauded, booed, written off and bounced back stronger than ever.

Let me put his career into context. Jason Leonard won 114 caps for England between 1990 and 2004, becoming everyone's favourite, the fun bus, the big boy next door, rightly seen as one of the immortal characters of English rugby. Mike Catt was an England player for only one year less than Leonard. He won 75 caps between 1994 to 2007.

That is a hell of a long time. It defies human levels of endurance, both physical and mental. Most internationals are lucky if they get four good years out of their bodies. Catt got 14 seasons. The man is superhuman. He adapted, he changed, he tweaked but at the core of it all was the simple fact that he was always superbly fit.

In the days when rugby training involved long runs, his three-kilometre time was close to nine minutes. That is lung-bustingly quick.

Neil Back was seen as a fitness freak. Catt was always there with him. His fitness-testing times in the old days were the benchmark, they were the special times to hit.

Jonny Wilkinson would follow the path blazed by Catty, but where you knew Wilkinson had punished himself to achieve such results, there was always a grace and naturalness to Mike's capacity to keep running, to keep working, to push himself and to better those that were viewed his equal.

On top of the physique was the pass I have talked about, and a kick that took time to develop and in the end was a joy to watch. He has a kicking swing any youngster would die for.

Relaxed, as if he is doing no work, producing a flight that is deadly accurate with a rifling spiral. He also never lacked courage, he never believed he would lose.

Retirement just means that his body, while not falling apart, had, at the age of 38, hit the end of the road to be competitive at the highest level. The gaps he still sees his body can no longer make. The tackles he can still visualise lack the power he once gave them. The brain is as sharp as ever and will continue to be for many years. It is just that I don't want to think of Cattman, my Cattman, as a coach.

That is not the image I will carry of him though. For me he is a rugby player, and I will remember him surrounded by others, before a match. Leonard is in a corner, Back patrolling as if he were a guard dog, Jason Robinson eerily quiet, Lawrence Dallaglio in full voice, Matt Dawson chipping away, Martin Johnson imploring. I am trying to relax. Catty has that fire in his eyes.

I thought he would go on forever, that I could live rugby through him, pretending that the clock was not ticking, that as long as one of us was playing, then we were still as young and as strong as ever.

But we aren't and with Catt gone, the curtain falls on a generation of three-quarters who straddled the amateur and professional eras.

Toulouse's unsung hero

Great sporting moments often happen in the last place you look. In his book *The Blind Side*, Michael Lewis talks about the position of left tackle in American football. The position is not about glory, it is not about running yardage or passing precision. It is about the little things.

The job of the left tackle is to protect the quarterback on his blind side. Get it right, and the star of the game is free to win matches. Get it wrong and he can end up in hospital.

In Lewis's words, the job of the left tackle is seemingly mundane, but when it is executed by one of the greats, such as John Ayers, 'to the few who knew, and watched, it was a thing of beauty'.

Small things, big impact, a low profile in the darkest corners and respect from those in the know for the job you do. The life of the left tackle could be a blueprint for the unsung heroes of the Heineken Cup. Over the past 15 years the best teams have all had them, the nameless men who give their all for the team, the players who ask for nothing more than game time and a club jersey.

But before I tell you who I am talking about, do a quick test with me. I know I've sprung this on you, and it's Saturday, but do me a favour and try this out. Think of it as interactive journalism.

How many players from the Toulouse team can you name? Put the paper down, try to work them out, then carry on reading. I bet some names came more easily than others. The back three of Vincent Clerc, Clément Poitrenaud and Cédric Heymans would have rolled off your tongue. Yannick Jauzion would be mentioned in the first breath. Byron Kelleher and Jean-Baptiste Elissalde would have got called early on.

In the forwards, Thierry Dusautoir, France's Grand Slam-winning captain, would be hard to forget. William Servat, perhaps the best hooker in the world, is a name most of us would recognise even if we couldn't place his face.

But I would be willing to bet considerable sums of hard-earned cash that the blind-side flanker for Toulouse never entered your mind. Even if I told you his name, you would probably have no idea who the hell he was and what he looked like. Which is a shame, because when Toulouse played in three consecutive finals from 2003 to 2005, and won two of them, he was there.

When they lost to Munster in 2008 he was there as well. And when they face Biarritz, he will be there.

His name is Jean Bouilhou and he is a Toulousain legend who is unknown by 99 per cent of rugby supporters. A one-club man, he has been at Toulouse since 1999. He is the rock which allows the Toulouse superstars to earn their plaudits and their sponsorship deals.

He has won caps for France, but only two, the last of which was in 2003. Bouilhou is a remarkably unremarkable player. And that is what makes him so special. From the look of it, God has not given him a physique that would allow him to compete in his tough position at such a high level for so long. He is lean, bony, light, and he even has grey hairs. He is not a powerhouse, a sprinter, or a strong man. He scores average marks in all these categories and yet he is a player the Toulouse coach, Guy Novès, cannot do without.

In the French Championship semi-final against Perpignan, with some players rested for the Heineken Cup final, Novès made him captain, sending his warrior out to try to achieve the impossible. All he had to do was beat the French champions with a second-choice front five and a fourth-choice scrum-half. Incredibly, he nearly pulled it off and, not content with that, Bouilhou even had a canter up the middle, a 40-metre run. It was the first time I had ever seen him in open space.

So why is he pivotal? He has the ability to read games, to be where the action is, to make the right calls, to have error-free matches, to know when to throw the speculative pass and when not to. He is always thinking. A player seemingly lacking in so many other departments, he has to use the grey matter more than most.

Nowhere is this more evident than in the line-out. This is where he shines. This is where Bouilhou dominates. He moves up and down the line-out taking the ball in every area.

Yet he is at his most valuable when Toulouse have a defensive line-out five metres from their own line. The opposition may know that the ball is going to Bouilhou, but they just cannot get anywhere near it. When the pressure is applied he is always up to the test, and in a tight match he is their man.

The opening line-out in the 2010 Heineken Cup semi-final against Leinster was only ever going to one man. And when the driving line-outs were used by Toulouse to such stunning effect, if he did not catch the ball then he was buried somewhere deep inside the morass of bodies, edging the maul forward, gaining valuable inches before the ball was sent hurtling out to the try-scoring machines behind.

There is something of the magnet about him when it comes to the ball. When it is loose on the deck, he secures it even if he does so in such an ugly, inflexible manner that you half-expect him to hobble off. At restarts he climbs high, with no thought for personal safety, trusting his team-mates to look after him. With ball in hand in confined spaces he smuggles it clear and offloads to bigger runners or whippet scrum-halves.

Against Leinster, he made short-yardage carries all day, picking off a yard here and a yard there, rarely dying with the ball and yet never going far enough with it for a neutral fan to ask 'who was that guy?' In the wide channels his defence was secure enough to pick off Brian O'Driscoll.

At the breakdown his discipline is exceptional. He competes, he steals, but if he cannot do something, then he is always listening for the referee or looking to roll away. He is a man a referee can trust.

And yet for all his positives, Bouilhou goes about his game a virtual unknown. A ghostly figure in a team of multi-coloured, star-spangled superstars. Nothing about him will have you cheering him on. He will not get you out of your seats in admiration, and to many it will seem as though he has no specific role. Don't believe your first impression.

Take the time to watch him more closely, because you will see a man who is never far from the ball, and who makes more telling contributions in every game than any of the superstars who surround him.

Jean Bouilhou is Toulouse's secret treasure. It would be great if the Heineken Cup could unearth many more just like him.

A poor diver but a great try-scorer

I know it's about the rugby and I shouldn't get drawn into the chat about 'that' dive or 'those' dives. But as someone who likes to see themselves as a try-scoring expert, it is difficult to bite your lip. I am not sure what all the fuss is about, because Chris Ashton is not very good at the try-scoring dive. The acceleration into the take-off is good. The balance to get there, the quick glance around to check that the runway is clear of any would-be tacklers; that is great. The one-armed signal to warn of the intent, to build us up mentally for what is about to come, that is outstanding.

Great athletes have used similar techniques. Mike Powell in Tokyo, Bob Beamon in Mexico, Carl Lewis in Los Angeles, they would, at this point of the dive, sit back in admiration. It's just that after this crescendo, it all goes downhill from there.

Strictly Come Dancing judge Len Goodman might at best give it a '7', Bruno Tonioli would gasp at the posture, then admit to feeling a little let down by the whole experience. And Craig Revel Horwood? He would just pull it apart. Ask Tom Daley if he ever makes a dive where his feet touch the water first. I bet he doesn't. And that is my problem. Ashton bottles his dives.

He is a diving coward. He doesn't hold his nerve and go the whole way. As he takes off you think it will be spectacular. And then, in mid-air, it becomes neither one thing nor the other. His feet trailing along, they break his speed and break his fall.

I know cowardly dives. At Cardiff in 2001 I came trotting around from left to right, approached the posts side on in the dead-ball area, and with the Millennium Stadium ready to be silenced, I went for lift-off, got scared before my body could come forward and landed on my feet in a rather pathetic skip. It taught me an important lesson: that you have to go all-in on a dive. Otherwise it detracts from what you are doing.

That is a huge shame for Ashton because he is a player doing things of which the rest of us can only dream. I put him in my World XV in 2010 to hoots of derision. But a fellow poacher can spot one a mile off. He sniffs out the line. He is a sniffer.

Let me highlight his fourth try against Italy in the 2011 Six Nations. It was almost full time, with an Italian throw at a line-out

10 yards from England's line. Ashton was on the goal line in the bottom right-hand corner, about as far away in terms of width as it is possible to be from Matt Banahan, who would eventually deliver the try-scoring pass. The ball is overthrown at the line-out, James Haskell delivers a pass to Jonny Wilkinson, the ball is shifted left. Gonzalo Canale in the Italian midfield is caught narrow.

Ashton is still right and out of the game. He's not even in the script, the same play, or act as the ball. So what would the average rugby player do when he realises this? He would run towards the ball. But not Ashton. From the moment Haskell first touched the ball, Ashton was off on his own track. When Mr Average went left, our sniffer headed on a diagonal for the corner flag at the far end.

The anticipation that the sniffer has tells him that the most likely situation for him to get into play would be to meet Banahan near the halfway line. There is no point running left – if he gets there and the ball is still there he can't help anyway. So the only chance of him touching the ball is to head on the diagonal to the halfway line. Most of England's support runners ended up left of Banahan as the winger moved back in from the touchline.

They were gone from the play, tucked in on Banahan's left as he is angling right. But not Ashton. The man who has run half the distance of the others still has the burst of speed in his legs to race away and score.

Unfortunately, it was all ruined by that poor dive. The coach needs to have a word. Not because Ashton is going to drop the ball. But because the way he's scoring tries we are going to have to watch that rubbish for years to come.

The real Austin Healey

Austin Healey is not someone everyone loves. He is a very polarising character. For me, though, he has always been a very close friend both during and after our playing careers. In 2008, Austin signed up for Strictly Come Dancing *and showed millions of TV viewers what the rest of us had always known – that there is more to the man than just the mouth.*

In a gym on one of Leicester's smaller back streets, Austin Healey is going through his dance training. I am there watching him, and so are the ghosts of his rugby past.

As he rumbas and salsas, the music turning his feet into twinkles, the spirit of the city's hard men look down on him. It's difficult to know what the likes of Martin Johnson, Dean Richards and Neil Back would make of it all. At one point Austin complains that he is 'not getting the transition between the promenade runs quite right', and I wonder what has become of us.

This is a man who called opposition players planks and would use his razor tongue to hurt anyone who dared challenge him. He was a funny guy but he had an edge.

He was someone who loved to exaggerate, and never missed an opportunity to tell you that he was the fastest winger in the Premiership, the best-paid player in the UK, and that he could unlock any defence.

The one-upmanship did not stop with the rugby and continued into his retirement. Only now he was the best poker player in the world with the best hair treatments and a unique brand of chat that was in demand from every reality TV show on air.

No one else comes close in the bragging stakes. Even the way he went about getting to the top of the rugby world was uniquely Austin. He cheated, punched, stamped, shouted, abused, and stalked his way up the ladder while the rest of his generation got their heads down, worked hard, spoke when spoken to, listened, learnt, and waited.

Not Austin – he knew it all from the get-go. He took no prisoners because he was hell-bent on being in a successful club and national team, and squeezing everything he could out of the game and his talent. He made friends – I was always his biggest fan. But he also made enemies, and I fear he made more of these in the latter days of his career.

What made it all the more galling was that his words were not merely empty boasts, he had the skills to put his outrageous claims into practice. He is one of the most talented rugby players this country will ever produce. While most of us were happy to focus on one position he represented his country at scrum-half, fly-half, wing and full-back.

That's just not something an ordinary person does. Clive Woodward made many great decisions in the build-up to the 2003 World Cup. One I think he got wrong was leaving this guy at home. But that's what happens when you say what you think all the time, people can no longer see past the chat and aggravation.

Nothing has changed in the 18 years that I have known him. Until *Strictly Come Dancing* came along, that is.

What has been so shocking about Austin on the show is that he seems so un-Austin-like. He is humble, polite, articulate. It is almost as if he has been replaced by a kinder twin brother. I want to find out what is going on, get to the bottom of why he seems to have mellowed and discover if ballroom dancing can really be the reforming factor. I have dressed for the occasion in a purple suit with yellow ruffled shirt.

Austin, for the record, is in a *Saturday Night Fever* ensemble that I picked up on my way through. He is the king of fancy dress – I remember seeing him and his wife having an argument outside a nightclub while he was dressed as a gorilla, she a polar bear – and I couldn't resist getting the disco gear on. I ask him if he has really changed, if he has become a new Austin.

He says not. 'While I was in the rugby world I had to have a persona that protected me from other things, a barrier. I have been retired for two years now. I have worked in an investment bank – you can't go and work in an investment bank and start swearing at people and taking the mickey out of them or you will just get the sack.'

So retirement changed him? Again he disagrees. 'This is who I always was. I was a complete fraud on the rugby field. I was two people, one on the field, one at home.'

For as long as I have known Austin, his parents and family have always had a central role in his life. Father to four girls, he is married to Louise, who has been with him from the beginning. Ashley, his sister, lives nearby in Leicester. His father Alan – a mustard-coloured coat-wearing legend – is spending more time near his children and grandkids since the death of his wife and Austin's mum, Denise, to cancer last year.

'One of the things for doing this show and for doing anything in life is you want to make your family proud. Playing rugby, climbing Everest next year, dancing on *Strictly Come Dancing*, not falling over and getting a decent score. If I make it to November I will be dancing on the first anniversary of my mum's passing. It will be difficult, but my mum was a strong woman. She would just have said "stop whingeing and get on with it".'

And that is exactly what Austin has been doing. I ask him if the dancing has helped him get over the disappointment of missing out on the World Cup squad in 2003 and not getting a winner's medal. 'If I won this, if I climbed Everest in a record time, I don't think it would ever take away the fact that I wasn't involved in that team. I had spent so long with all those guys prior to it and I had got injured just at the wrong time.'

So I ask if he is trying to prove something on *Strictly*, show that he can go one better than the show's only other rugby contestant and long-time rival Matt Dawson?

'This dancing has nothing to do with trying to prove other people wrong or make a statement about myself. Those days are gone. The days when you had to make a statement and stand up in a big man's world, I couldn't really give a shit anymore – it doesn't matter to me. This is about my family enjoying an experience and me being part of it.'

So does he reckon he can win the competition? 'I genuinely have not thought about winning it. You can't allow yourself to. Just like the old rugby days, it's game by game, Saturday by Saturday. I think there are eight or six people who could realistically win it.'

By now I am having difficulty hanging on to reality. Austin has just passed up a chance to tell me how the show is his to win, how he dances better than Fred Astaire and Ginger Rogers combined. My jaw is on the floor. The only time he brags at all during the day is when he jokingly says that anyone from the current series could have won in Matt Dawson's year. There is a small sudden glimmer of the old Austin, but it is gone almost as quickly as it appears.

The only sparks I see in Leicester are between Austin and his dancing partner Erin. He is quick, sharp, she is lithe and graceful. Kicks, swaying hips, strong arms. Some rumba, in and out of styles. Then the routine starts, a mistake, start again.

Halfway through, mistake, start again. Erin barks out orders, 'on your toes', 'head up', 'snap the arms', 'legs straight', 'don't jump'. Constant mentoring and hectoring from Erin.

In the old days Austin would have said poke it, now he resigns himself to being told what to do. When he gets it wrong, Erin takes his hand and leads him back to the start like a naughty schoolboy, and off they go again. Bobbing and weaving, Austin looks like a boxer, and the words of Muhammad Ali spring to mind: 'The fight is won or lost far away from witnesses – behind the lines, in the gym, and out there on the road, long before I dance under those lights.'

The lips from Louisville and Leicester, never known for their modesty but never afraid of hard work. And Austin is putting in the graft. When I was there, he and Erin danced for six hours. There are new dances to learn each week, technical difficulties, differing styles.

At the beginning of the day the steps are alien to him and there is not a hint of a smile. Soon, however, the steps come good and the cheeky grin that used to accompany his searing breaks and try-scoring celebration routines returns. Austin emerges from his shell. By the end of their day rehearsing the samba, a dance that usually requires seven mojitos before any normal man will attempt it, he is moving those hips and ready for a carnival.

There have been many exaggerations about Austin Healey, most self-proclaimed. But there have also been many misunderstandings. It would be funny if dancing and not rugby lets us see what he is really made of.

A complicated competitor

Colin Montgomerie is not a man who fails to get a reaction. Ryder Cup legend, Scottish hero, miserable sod, petulant kid, sponsor's dream, outspoken troublemaker, candidly honest. Wherever he goes there is action, reaction, comment, jibe, support, hostility.

For years I have been fascinated by the man, not least because of his sporting abilities. In the Ryder Cup I have applauded his role as the ultimate team player in a singularly single-minded sport. When he is on his own, I have watched him finish runner-up five times in a major. He played some magnificent golf along the way but always fell short, critics claiming he never had the mental strength to close out a big one.

Yet he was tough enough and good enough to top the European Tour's Order of Merit every year from 1993 to 1999, a record unbroken run as No 1. He has inspired a generation of golfers, so why is it that so many negative stories seem to follow him around?

I am as guilty as anyone because when I think of Monty I do not remember his triumphs, I remember his biggest disappointment – the 2006 US Open. On the last hole of the tournament, Monty had one hand on the trophy. He drove perfectly from the tee, finding position A. There was then a delay of a few minutes as his playing partner, Phil Mickelson, hacked around in the marquees, and in a now-famous change of mind, Monty switched from a six-iron to a seven for his approach shot.

He hit it badly, came up short, chipped on, three-putted from 30 feet and handed the title to Australia's Geoff Ogilvy.

As a human being you sympathise. As a sportsman you want to

know what went on in his head during that delay. What demons came at him, what voices did he have to fight down, why was his usually fluid, long backswing suddenly so short?

He has, by common consent, a complicated personality. I watched Monty play the last few holes of his third round at the Open in 2008 at Royal Birkdale. Follow him and you pick up mutterings of 'grumpy' and 'moody' among the crowd. There are acidic rumours that mobile phones have been banned at his request. And yet when Monty approaches the greens or tees, the crowd roar their approval from all sides, making it clear that he is loved.

In the quiet moments you watch him talk to his caddie. He looks for reassurance over yardage on a long approach to the 17th green. The bagman steadily repeats: 'The carry is 222, get it in the air.'

Happy, convinced, buying into it, Monty commits fully to the shot. And when he does there is nothing more languid than the Scot fading one off the tee, or stroking a long iron. Only Fred Couples could look more relaxed.

However, the easy manner dissolves on the green as he putts for a birdie and the ball stays out of the hole. Monty blames 'a big gust of wind'. The marshal behind me adds: 'He'll be smashing his putter – yesterday it was his driver.'

There is more to come on the final hole, by which time he is 11 over par for the tournament. The press corps get a little too close, and he moves them on in a less-than-courteous manner.

Then, while standing over his second shot on the 18th, he suddenly steps away. The caddie reassures him that he has the right club but that is not the problem. The difficulty is 'marshals moving all over the place behind the green – standard issue'.

I look into the distance and see that the distraction is more than 200 yards away. It is a championship weekend, there are 50,000 visitors to be kept in check, surely he can understand that the marshals are just doing their job? And why is something so far away affecting him so badly when he is already 11 over par?

These are the questions that rattle around my brain as I drive to meet Monty and play 18 holes with him in a pro-am at the Belfry. I am overjoyed at the chance to see him in action close-up, but I am also nervous about which Monty will turn up – the charmer or the snarler?

The man I meet is open, thoughtful and talkative. He is aware of his public persona and admits, with a laugh, that he does care what people think. 'You see me around and I am not that way,' he said. 'I'm trying possibly too hard in what I do as a living. It's unfortunate that I can't hide behind a helmet that a cricketer can wear. It's out there, it's open.'

But what about the tensions he often said existed between his life on and off the course? 'I am happier now the way it's set up, between the joy and the hobby of the game. And the competitiveness of it. It's nice to know when you start a round of golf that you don't have to prove anything to anyone. That's been done. So I go out and I am actually enjoying the game much more than I ever did.

'Everything's in order, the business side of things – it's going well off the course. So I can really come to these tournaments and enjoy myself. I have a smile on my face on the first tee.'

He certainly seems happy. He dives into bunkers to give playing partners impromptu lessons, sees my old golf glove and gives me three new ones, signs every autograph, poses for every photo, cracks jokes, and says he likes Coldplay so much that when he saw them at Earl's Court, he went back the following night to watch them again.

In between shots he talks about his mother, Elizabeth, who died in 1991, and of how he is setting up a lung cancer centre in Glasgow in her memory and trying to raise £5.2 million to roll others out across Scotland. He extols the virtues of his Lexus hybrid car as though it were a close friend. He is just another bloke sharing a laugh and golf-course banter.

The only time I see any sign of more difficult, deeper emotions is when I bring up that shot in the US Open and ask why it went wrong. 'Tension. This was my chance after being runner-up so many times. I did mess up, yes. And I regret it, and will regret it, if I don't win one. That's the shot . . . every time I draw the seven-iron out of my bag I think "Oh—".'

You can see it still smarts, but Monty isn't giving up just yet. 'I am exempt on the European Tour until I'm 52, which is 2015. I've got seven years left and I look forward to playing in them. Do I enjoy golf? No. Do I enjoy the competition? Yes. The range days, hitting the balls, the golf, no. I don't get up about hitting a three-iron onto the green with a big, high draw. I just think, "Great that's close, I can now hole the putt to beat the competitor I'm playing against."'

Has that always been the case? 'It used to be more of a search for perfection within the game, now it's a competition. I love the competition, but the golf, not so much.'

Honest to a fault, and maybe that has been Monty's Achilles heel. While so many others are schooled in the sound bite, he just says it as he sees it. During our chat, and in interviews with other journalists, he talks about the Ryder Cup and Europe's thumping defeat.

His comments appear in newspapers as an attack on Nick Faldo and his captaincy. This was harsh on Monty. He was not being a troublemaker, he was speaking his mind.

I come from a team sport where troublemakers were often ostracised, yet you need people with conviction and passion, who believe in what they do, to speak up.

I ask Monty if he regrets some of his outbursts and behaviour over the years. 'Everyone regrets incidents in their time of 20 years in front of the camera. But at the same time it's just me giving 110 per cent,' he says.

This commitment is what makes Monty the man he is, both good and bad, and it is what draws us to him. We live his highs and suffer his lows and by the end of my time that bloody seven-iron even has me swearing.

Madness and Malbon

In 2009 I got a chance to see what it was like to be a round-the-world sailor – a taller Northern version of Dame Ellen MacArthur. The race that made her famous was the Vendée Globe and the man who was stepping up to try and win it in 2009 offered to take me for a spin.

Boat masts are deceptively tall. Sit near the top of one, 80 feet in the air, and you get a fresh perspective on the sport of single-handed sailing.

The boat was in the dock, the water was as still as a millpond, and there was not a breath of air. And yet, I swear, it was swaying about like a television antenna in a hurricane. The sea looked miles away and I just wanted to come down. No chance.

Up there with me was Jonny Malbon and he is made of sterner

stuff. Spare a thought for Jonny at lunchtime on Sunday. While the rest of us settle down for a roast, some drinks and an afternoon snooze, this seafaring lunatic will set off on the biggest event in solo yachting, the Vendée Globe.

If the name rings bells, that's because it is the race Dame Ellen MacArthur so nearly won. Remember her tears and suffering?

It is a competition of mind-boggling endurance, where sailors are alone for three months and cannot get any outside help, nor set foot on land for the entire duration.

Their home for that time is a 60-foot monohull racing yacht that is pared down for speed, and built for the toughest of seas. Imagine strapping yourself into a Formula One sports car and then getting out three months later and you have some idea of what they are putting themselves through.

The Vendée starts and finishes in Les Sables d'Olonne, France, and the course will take the sailors round the three great capes marking the southern tips of Africa, Australia and South America.

For those of us outside of the sailing community it is difficult to understand the lure of this race. In France, the contestants are national heroes. On Sunday there are expected to be 500,000 people lining the shore to watch the Vendée's 30 sailors heading off.

When I visit Les Sables d'Olonne, a small port with a museum dedicated to shellfish, there are thousands of visitors day and night. There is a rolling video on the harbour wall showing a montage of the race's most famous moments. At night there is a blaze of green and purple lights, and spotlights rake the sky.

Tied to their piers, the boats look sleek and powerful, £60 million worth of pent-up technology waiting to be unleashed. The men and women who will pilot these racehorses of the sea are just as extraordinary.

In 1968, the first round-the-world non-stop Golden Globe was eventually won by Sir Robin Knox-Johnston in 312 days.

Frenchman Bernard Moitessier, who had been leading, passed a cargo ship in the South Atlantic and shot a message to it with a catapult. It read: 'I'm heading on to the Pacific Islands because I am so happy here at sea, and maybe also to save my soul.' He then headed for Polynesia.

It was also the race in which amateur sailor Don Crowhurst disappeared at sea, having reported false positions. Since Knox-Johnston's victory, the French have dominated the sport of solo navigations and are convinced they will do so again.

Standing in their way is Malbon, a 34-year-old from Cowes who is in the process of fattening up prior to his departure and will be taking 2,000 cigarettes with him on his journey.

'I have sailed since I was five. My old man was in the Navy and we went to France for five weeks every summer, sailing. I always loved it.'

But it wasn't a career for him and years ago, while his two brothers were at university, Malbon worked as a DJ on the London club scene. Figuring it had a limited shelf life, he started to take sailing more seriously and moved to Cowes on the Isle of Wight. He has never looked back.

It was a steady progression, teaching dinghy sailing on the side to pay the bills, as he worked his way up to bigger and faster boats. Ambitious as it must have seemed, the Vendée Globe was always his goal. Malbon tells me that he has been 'training forever for this'.

The wind and boat skills he has today, he started picking up as a five-year-old. Every time he fixed something, broke it and had to fix it again has been part of his learning process. Every day spent on a boat, no matter what type, has been an education. And he will need to rely on everything he has learnt because once the race starts, Malbon is on his own.

He has watched his boat, *Artemis Ocean Racing II*, grow from nothing and he has been there every step of the way. He knows how to take apart and reassemble every component of every piece of equipment, from engine to watermaker.

He must be jack of all trades. And it is not just the equipment that will be under incredible pressure.

In the first few days of the race, as the boats scramble for position in heavy shipping lanes, Malbon's alarm will go off every 10 minutes of every hour of every day.

If he is lucky he will be able to hit the snooze button and grab 20 minutes' kip. His bean-bag-cum-bed, the sort you would find in a student flat, is positioned near his computer where his dials tell him everything that is going on.

He doesn't like the bunks in the side of the boat as they are too far from the control panel. On deck, luxury is also in short supply. The space is about five square metres, and the grinding machine, which hoists the huge sails up and down, takes centre stage.

There are two great big steering wheels on either side, some levers on ground level that can be changed with your feet and two sets of screens feeding information about wind, speed and other sailing statistics.

The whole front deck of the carbon-fibre shell has a sandpaper effect for grip. Malbon says the idea is to be strapped on to something whenever you go up front; in reality, he tells me, life is different.

Near the winching machine there is what looks like a mass of ropes, a thousand snakes writhing together. Colour coded, they make some sense when he explains what they do. However, it is the mast that dominates everything.

It is here that success or failure will hang. Dismasting is a sailor's worst nightmare, their boat turns from a racing machine into a wallowing weight. Malbon is aware of the dangers, but says they don't get to him, even when things are going wrong.

'I can't be scared,' he argues, 'because I have never been to some of these godforsaken places.'

His support team are a little less blasé. Christophe Baudry, the Vendée Globe director of communications, explains exactly where the sailors are heading.

'The Southern Ocean is more isolated than the moon,' he says.

'From the moon it takes three days to get back. In the South Seas you rely on yourself or your competitors behind you, no one can turn back to help you.'

His girlfriend of five years is Blandine Chemineau, a marketing executive on the *Artemis* team. She is having to deal with her own emotions in the lead-up to the race.

'I am scared for him, but also very happy for him. This is his dream. When he wants something he does everything he can to make it happen.'

As I chat to Malbon on board *Artemis* there is activity everywhere. A Frenchman with a knife has been hired to help with some rigging. The rest of the race team are checking, rechecking, and checking the equipment again.

The team of Graham 'Gringo' Tourell, Ian 'Mucky' McCabe, Gareth 'Nipper' Rowley, Rob and Scottie are swarming over the boat.

I ask Malbon how important this back-up is to his race. He says he is lucky that they are all mates, who can tell instantly what he is thinking. He says he will call Gringo every day, and that the chat will be a mental release.

However, he doesn't want to spend too long talking to people on land as that can be painful.

Malbon tells of the time that Blandine, who hides little packages on the boat to cheer him up in dark times, once fell asleep while on the phone to him. It was during a massive party at his home, and all he could hear while he was at sea was everyone having a great night.

'Christmas will be the worst time,' he reckons. 'I can't think of anything worse than putting on a Santa hat and pretending to be having a good time.'

Depending on his luck, he may be back quickly. He plans to do the race in 85 to 90 days. Anything less would be brilliant. However, he must be careful not to sail the boat to pieces. It is a long race and he will try not to get caught up in 'a smoking start'. The one thing he is prepared for is madness.

During his qualification sails, Malbon started hallucinating. He kept seeing a guy from Cowes poking his head out of the cabin, and constantly heard someone shout 'Roger, ready'. After three weeks, he caught himself shouting out the phrase 'not sure about that, mate'.

Malbon says he will fight the voices and his comments confirm what I was already thinking when I saw him bouncing around at the top of the mast.

To do the Vendée requires a certain amount of lunacy and a complete disregard for personal safety. And yet it makes perfect sense when you hear him talk of his love for the sea and sailing.

It's a solo sport that is impossible to do without the help of others, where your very survival may depend on rivals giving up their own ambitions to pull you from the raging seas. Malbon says that he is ready to pit his wits against the seas.

A Diet Coke and a smoke

I lay flat on my back, there was a sense of excitement, bewilderment and terror at what was about to unfold. How does a leisurely round of golf end up with a tee peg in your mouth, a ball precariously balanced on top of it and John 'the Wild Thing' Daly winding up for a life-threatening swing?

Daly had me all ends up. The teeth were rattling so much that the ball only ever stayed in place for two or three seconds. The practice swings swooshed by so close that I could hear my bones whistle.

And then finally, the sphincter-relaxing laughter that broke out when he realised my massive conk meant he could not get a clean hit of the ball. I always knew my nose would come in handy. Welcome to the Daly World.

Whatever your understanding of golf and its quaint rules, a round with John Daly suggests there is a parallel universe out there.

It was a wet and blustery day when I met up with him. As we lined up for the pro-am day at the European Open, out of the haze, down the middle of the 18th fairway came the Wild Thing, fag at a jaunty angle, waterproofed up, hat down over his ears.

Whatever it is cool dudes have, he has it in spades. You are drawn to him and I feel like a schoolkid again. He doesn't waste any time chatting. The 1995 Open champion just stands on the tee and smashes the ball straight down the middle, 300 yards. A minute later, the starter's shotgun goes off telling everyone it's OK to start their round.

Daly has gone well before the B of the bang. He goes when he is ready, and you better be able to keep up. He almost takes a run-up at each shot and if he could he would be round the course, any course, in 2½ hours. Slow play is what really winds him up and it is what gets his goat on days like these.

For starters, it is far too cold and wet, and then there is the hanging around on each tee, waiting for the amateurs who want to hole out on every hole. Hit six on a hole and you're better off picking the ball up, otherwise you feel he might ram it down your throat. For all his smiles and wisecracks, there is a brooding menace that simmers near the surface.

But while he might sometimes snarl, it is a svelte John Daly that I am playing with. He has lost 60 pounds in four months since he had his new-style stomach band fitted. Twenty-eight pounds in the first month. He is not an Olympic athlete and I must admit I was thinking what the hell he must have looked like before the band.

However, the healthy lifestyle has not quite seen him give up the fags. I ask him if he carries anything unusual in his golf bag. He replies that the first things he puts in are his cigarettes and lighter fuel.

The clubs come later. He smokes the strong Marlboro Reds as well, no messing about with Lights. Does he start each day with one? No, the caffeine from the Diet Coke comes first, then the nicotine. Not a bad combo to start your day.

In our five-hour round, the only time he gets really upset is when Nick Hibbs, his representative from the club sponsor, Adams, brings his Diet Coke two hours after he had asked for it.

But after a quick slug, the smile is back. You have the feeling if he wants to get really angry, he could be scary. Yet the moment it has all passed by, it would be forgotten about.

Instead, what you marvel at the whole way round is his apparent lack of effort and the languid swing that almost touches his toes on the way back, the cigarette always near his lips.

At one stage he hits a four-iron into the breeze with no practice swing and with a cigarette pluming smoke into his face. It goes 195 yards and ends up four feet from the hole.

His speed of play is frightening. I'm repairing my pitch mark on a short par three and am about to congratulate myself for hitting a green John had missed, when I realise that he has already chipped in behind me and is walking to the next tee.

His putter and clubs have enormous, giant grips. They look like baseball bats. He seems to have 23 different clothing outfits. His main range of clothes is his Loudmouth brand – pants that take colours to the extreme. He says he is now looking to move into women's clothing, and would love to design a range of G-strings.

When we talk about his boozing, he says he 'does' whisky now as he can't 'do' beers. He explains that he is from Arkansas. Not the place where Dorothy tapped her shoes and hoped to get back to in *The Wizard of Oz*, but the state where 'Slick' Bill Clinton comes from.

He laughed at life, love and death and made fun of illnesses and the world's need for Viagra. With his silly humour, Daly made our whole group feel good about ourselves.

Funny, illuminating, odd, inspiring, John Daly manages to cram a whole host of personalities into his massive frame. Strangely, steady pro golfer is the one that seems the least like who he really is.

Christmas treats

There are certain things at Christmas that are non-negotiable. Turkey, presents for the kids, something nice for the wife, and darts on the telly.

I love it. The voice of Sid Waddell soothes me and his lines, 'That was like throwing three pickled onions into a thimble', 'Look at the man go, it's like trying to stop a water buffalo with a peashooter', make my holidays for me.

The atmosphere, the noisy excitable crowd, the tension. It's what makes the sport great.

And standing at the top of it all is Phil Taylor. Fourteen world championships and he still has plenty of juice left in the tank.

Over the holidays, the Greenwood family stays up as one, watching as 'The Power' caresses his arrows into the board, treble after treble after treble. So you can imagine my nerves when I get offered the chance of playing against Phil.

Do not be fooled into thinking that you can just turn up and give it a crack. Taylor is the Vijay Singh of darts. He spends hour upon hour upon hour striving for perfection. Just like Daley Thompson used to, he will be practising on Christmas Day.

I am a long way off this. Also, I am not sure what to expect of Phil. I've never met a darts player before. I have no clue what they are like. His answerphone message is hilarious.

'Hello, this is Phil, if you can't get hold of me it's because Barry Hearn has got me working again, like a bloody slave I am.'

When there are press interviews it is Taylor everyone wants to talk to, and with it you sense there must be some animosity from his fellow pros as he hoovers up the prize money and the sponsorship deals.

It's easy to forget that this is a man who used to hold down three jobs so that he could play darts, who used to travel the world with nothing, hoping he would win the tournament so that he could pay off some debts.

In the early days, he was sponsored by the great Eric Bristow. 'When Alexander of Macedonia was 33, he cried salt tears because there were no more worlds to conquer . . . Bristow's only 27'. Waddell again, referring to Bristow at the height of his career.

When Taylor met the Cockney legend, his abilities were on the wane hampered by dartitis, the ailment which meant Bristow couldn't let go of the darts at the right time. However, the timing was spot on for Taylor, who ended up being sponsored by Bristow. He would travel, get the bills picked up by the former champion and when he won, he handed the money over to his backer.

For Taylor it was a lifeline, even if it meant he had very little money and lived on boiled ham and crisps from the local shop. And it meant that Bristow was on his back all the time about practising, not wanting to see his money wasted.

While it was a tough way to learn, it instilled in Taylor an old-school sense of respect and a hard-work ethic that has pushed him to where he is today. He is a superstar in a sport that harks back to working men's clubs and smoky pubs.

So, if I am honest, I was a bit confused about who I would be meeting. Down-to-earth bloke from Stoke or arrogant world beater? He arrived at the Park Lane Hilton in London wearing a trainspotter's jacket, helped by an assistant who was clearly just a mate. He looked a little bit like a postman.

Then, in a flash, the coat comes off and he is standing there in a shirt with all the sponsors' logos on and, more importantly, 'The

Power' written bold across the back. And with it comes the change in his eyes. Like Clark Kent, he has gone from the bloke next door to a killer tungsten Superman.

I feel like a fool in my darts shirt with Will 'Rodney Trotter' Greenwood on the back. This guy is going to bury me. At the oche, his eyes fix on the target like a laser.

Everything else is shut out. He stands with his foot side on to the oche, the flight brushes right back to his nose and then the lazy arm, the relaxed follow through, the dart hitting its target with just about enough power to pierce the board.

Commentators call it stacking, so he can parachute the next dart in over the top. Taylor's darts seem to defy gravity, weighing in at just 26 grams, they jut downwards from the board at about 35 degrees, clinging on, awaiting the arrival of their pal next to them.

At the dartboard The Power is a machine. In full flow he is unstoppable. There is no superstition with this guy either. If he plays eight matches in a tournament he uses eight different sets of darts. As they clatter into each other time and again, the grooves get worn, the weight dipping slightly.

He has used heavier darts, and is not afraid to tinker. Look at his flights and you can see that they read 'The Dower' because he has cut them down, and with it the bottom of the P, with a pair of nail scissors. Forget the super-shoes that Usain Bolt uses, or the magic swimsuits that have broken world records.

There is no laser guidance, or scientific conditions for The Power – he just trims when and what he needs. And it works. He told me he has won £250,000 since he cut them down. All the time we practise, there's banter. I want to hear stories of accidental shoulder-barging opponents, of sledging, but he says it doesn't happen.

The crowd do that for you, and he doesn't care what his opponent does. He just focuses on getting to his double as quickly as he can. He tells me, matter of factly, that he had a nine-darter in the morning before meeting up with me.

And that is what it's all about for Phil. He loves the game. He played when he was young 'because there was no television in the house, so it was always cards, dominoes and darts'.

But he didn't really start playing the game until he began going to clubs with his dad. It was in Ryan Hall, the local Roman Catholic club, at the age of 12 that an old fella once told him he would be the best player in the world. It was the same club that Robbie Williams, Stoke's other famous son, first sang in.

Then, as so often happens, life got in the way, and Phil stopped playing darts. He worked in a factory, did up cars, and tried to make a living. It was only when he was 25, after watching an exhibition match with Bristow playing, that his wife bought him a set of darts. He joined a league and one night turned into two, two into three, and before he knew it, he was chucking seven days a week.

At first it was just a way to make a few hundred quid here and there, so he could buy something for the house, some curtains, saucepans or a carpet. But then he got better, and the game suddenly took off. My boss at Sky, Martin Turner, can take some of the credit for the rebirth of darts as he introduced the music, the girls, the super slo-mos and gave The Power his nickname.

It was after a drunken game of cribbage, and was linked to the song, 'The Power' by Snap! He could hardly have chosen a better moniker for the man who would go on to dominate the sport.

At the moment there is £5 million a year in the prize-money coffers of professional darts. By this time next year it may be £10 million. Taylor has won 25 per cent of this year's available loot alone.

The man who had very little, now has a lot. Darts has been good to him. He has bought houses, loving bricks and mortar as an investment. Phil tells me that if he wins the world championship again this year, he will buy another house.

While he may have more now than he ever thought he would, he is generous with his advice as well. In a small hotel room in London, he immediately comes up with tips, and tweaks.

And then comes the moment that will live with me for the rest of my life. He lent me his darts, and under the spotlight, the first time I threw with Phil Taylor's arrows, I hit a treble 20. It was like the dart was on remote control. The next dart dropped low, down to 17.

The final one, after adjusting to the new swing, no word of a lie, went into the treble 20 again. I threw 137. With Phil Taylor's darts.

It took him four more sets of three to better my score. I doubt he will be so kind to the opponents he meets in the world championship. To quote Waddell one final time: 'They won't just have to play outta their skin to beat Phil Taylor. They'll have to play outta their essence!'

A horsewoman extraordinaire

Giving a horse a bath is a delicate act. It requires a mix of friendly approach and firm handling. Not least when you are dealing with the sensitive parts of a very well-bred animal who in all likelihood will be carrying one of Britain's best medal hopes in the 2012 London Olympics. I was lucky in two respects.

First, I had Mary King, horsewoman extraordinaire, overseeing me. Second, her horse, Imperial Cavalier, or Archie as he is better known, was feeling ticklish. That meant our soapy bonding session was cut short before I got a kick in the head. Not that King was particularly worried. She just told me to 'give it a bit of ooom-mphh'. It was a phrase that would ring out regularly during my day with King. Any half-hearted effort at mucking out, grooming, riding, was always met with the reminder to get stuck in. She does not do things by halves.

Especially when she is preparing for the Burghley Horse Trials, which start on Thursday. Oh yes, she can sit around the table with her daughter Emily and mother Jill, offering lemon cake that is to die for and passing round cups of tea with the hospitality that you would expect from delicate ladies. But don't be fooled. These women have steel running through them – King's septuagenarian mother Jill drives the horse box up and down the tight bends that lead to their picture-perfect farm.

These are flint-eyed competitors and scrappers who would take you down if they had to. Look around their home and you see sporting equipment scattered around the place; rugby boots, cricket gear, hockey sticks, tennis balls, table tennis bat, squash rackets. This is my kind of place.

Sports photos don't cover every wall. Instead it's Mary meeting the Queen, Diana Princess of Wales, the young princes, the Princess Royal, and in among them a set of five photos, perhaps a gentle reminder of the courage needed to do what she does. Taken in 1988, they show a tumble and a horse flattening King, then a shot of her sitting up, helmet askew, looking winded and shocked as her horse scrambles to hoof. These are the photos of which King is most proud.

I don't know much about horses except to say that if one sat on me, I would not go back for more. For King this is part of the challenge, and when she talks of her sport, she says that the urge to compete, to push herself and the horse, is stronger than ever.

When I suggest she has incredible courage she slaps me down.

'No not at all. There are nerves; it is a challenging sport, that's what makes it so exciting. The challenge that lies ahead, especially in the cross-country. But I would only ride a horse around a course that I know is perfectly capable of jumping it . . . I must approach fences with the correct speed and the right amount of power but all my horses can do all the courses I put in front of them.'

So is it the horse or rider that is special? Zara Phillips knows what it takes to make it to the top. When I asked about King, she used the word unique. Mainly it was her style of riding, very backward in the saddle, long reins, but gets the job done.

Yet it was also about King's personality. 'She has a great amount of respect from everyone within the sport. Independently driven, and knows what she wants. But always makes you feel part of the team. A great team player.'

So, Mary King, a rare mix of tough loner and team player. You can certainly see her grit in how she got into the sport. Born to a quiet rural family, she started riding thanks to a kind local vicar who allowed her to use his pony. She fell in love, begged her parents and finally got her own horse, leaving school early to dedicate herself to her sport. She has cleaned old people's homes, she has delivered meat for the local butcher, she has done what she had to do.

Today King's success has brought her some respite in the shape of loyal sponsors to whom she is incredibly grateful. But the awareness that backers can come and go has made her a sharp horse trader and breeder. I learnt of flushing embryos, of surrogate mares, of schooling horses so that King can sell them on.

I learnt that the one thing she always tries to write into her contracts is that she can retain the ride on the horses as they grow up. She doesn't own horses in her own yard. There is an emotional detachment about this. She can't afford to keep pets. They are too expensive. I can believe that, and if I come back in another life I want to come back as one of King's horses. They are the Formula One machines, international sprinters, world-class footballers of the animal world.

Nothing is left to chance, especially as there is now more money splashing about. In order to have horses who can win, the preparation, the rest, the training routines, the personal hygiene, the diet needs to expertly controlled. The breakfast is weighed, measured and tailored to each horse. Half a teaspoon of salt for some; elastin for the joints of others; water cleaned out and swapped, and my first error of the day. I got some haylage in the water – bad start, ticking off taken. Then the mucking out.

These guys don't get straw, they get cut-up cardboard to ensure a dust-free environment and clear lungs. Their bed, in their immaculate stable, looked more comfortable than the one I have at home. King won't accept anything less than perfection, and this extends to the training she puts the horses through. I watch as two of them are raced full tilt up a ridiculous ascent. They pause at the top, then walk back down, repeating it four times. Classic anaerobic training.

Horses, it seems, are just like the rest of the athletes. There was a bit of a female Heathcliff about King as she set off up the hill into the mist, fog, and towards the trees, a lady on a passionate mission.

Would it burn so bright that she will look past the London Olympics and hang on until 2016? Does she hope that she and her daughter could make the same team? 'If I feel like I do now I will definitely be giving Rio a go in 2016.' Then she turns her attention to the Land Rover Burghley Horse Trials and the Clint Eastwood eyes return. I too decide that it's best to focus on riding, not least because I was about to get in the saddle for the first time in my life.

King was never going to allow a novice like me on one of her stars. No they needed something sturdy, something calm, something used to buffoons. Enter the half tank, half cow that will forever be my friend, Fergie. Shame on you Emily King for laughing at my horse. Shame on your whole yard for mocking my trusty companion. On I hopped in unglamorous style and we walked to the field where Mary practises show jumping and dressage.

A couple of stark truths sank in as we walked. I suddenly realised that it was a long way down, and that if Fergie really wanted to do something, there was very little I could do to stop her short of hanging on and screaming. The giggles all around didn't help. Helmets have never suited me. But before I could back out, we were in the arena and Mary turned all professional. Stood in the middle, with a rope on Fergie, she made us walk round in circles, changing from walk to trot to canter. Walk was OK, trot was interesting, canter was ohdeargodholdonfordearlife.

But we weren't stopping there. When I say we, I mean Mary. Off came the rope, round the arena, sitting trot, rising trot, walk, keep to the outsides, change reins, back straight, all sound easy when I write them but crikey back there the adrenalin pumped through me. And then, the grand finale, a jump of at least two feet. My first one. My last one. My Horse of the Year moment. From novice to jumper in 15 minutes. And if Mary King can do that, there really is nothing that she can't achieve.

Rugby Can Take You To Places You've Never Been

Magnificent sevens

In 2007 I travelled to Dubai for one of the best parties in the game, the Dubai Sevens. But amid the fun there was some serious rugby and glimpses of future stars.

Sevens has always had a funny standing in the global game. In the past, it has been the end-of-season runabout that let the youngsters off the leash and gave the older forwards a freedom they seldom got in the more adult world of 15-a-side. But as rugby has moved into the realms of professionalism, so too has sevens, even if it has still managed to hang on to its somewhat split personality.

Take the Dubai Sevens as a case in point. A serious tournament, but also one of the greatest rugby parties on the planet, it is a mix of amateur rubbish and professional genius, of honed bodies and wobbly bellies. I was lucky enough to attend last week as part of a team representing the Christina Noble Children's Foundation. At my age, it was not the main event that beckoned, rather the 10-a-side games that were organised for veterans.

There are very few people that the boots would come back on for, but getting the opportunity to run out once more with Allan Bateman, my midweek Lions co-centre from South Africa in 1997, was too much to resist.

Alongside us were the likes of Junior Tonu'u from the All Blacks,

Garrick Morgan of Australia, Craig Polla-Mounter, a rugby league Grand Final winner with the Canterbury Bulldogs, and three Welsh lads all called Evans. Jason Leonard and Sean Fitzpatrick were also lurking on the sidelines, enjoying the atmosphere, rehydrating in the desert heat and mingling with supporters.

The superstar professional sevens players from Fiji, New Zealand, South Africa and England all arrive a week in advance, spend time with local schools, sleep and fine-tune their skills. The rest of us get in a day or so before kick-off, and try not to worry about how we will survive one of the ultimate fitness tests that rugby has to offer. While the big boys are stretching, we are soaking up the carnival atmosphere and heading off to the biggest party of the week the night before our opening three games.

The smaller tournaments begin on Thursday, with colts, ladies and veterans all getting a go. We kicked off against Bishop's Stortford Old Boys and finished the day against some rather cantankerous older Russians. It's difficult to know what to do when a 50-year-old Ruskie hits you late and then gives you that 'I am old enough to be your dad' look when you seek retribution. Still, we got the job done and set up a quarter-final date with Swansea Old Boys on the Friday, when the main tournament began.

Come the opening day proper, the tone is very, very different. The 35,000-seat stadium is full by 9 a.m. and the atmosphere hots up quicker than the plastic seating. On the pitch it is helter-skelter, with supercharged hits and turbo-speed fliers. The Kiwis make it look so easy, the Fijians are laid-back, the English toil and graft. South African players seem as though they are chiselled from granite, while the Kenyans look like good milers as well as sprinters.

The sevens style of play mirrors, to a certain extent, that of the full international teams and is now the breeding ground for some serious talent. England went oh so close to turning the form book on its head in the semi-finals, when they were within a video referee's decision of beating Fiji. It was no fluke.

In their sweeper, Ben Foden, they have a great young player, while if Anthony Elliott's form was anything to go by, then there is another potential flier about to emerge in much the same way that David Strettle and Tom Varndell did from the sevens circuit.

In the front row of the sevens team is Tom Guest, a back-row forward at Harlequins who is quicker than most international centres, and could follow James Haskell to international recognition after schooling in the shorter-game arena.

For the cream of the crop, these tournaments are now a way of showing off, and proving to selectors that they have the skills needed to move into the main shop window of 15-a-side. For the rest of us, it is a chance to show we still have something left in the tank even if it is running low and our legs are becoming increasingly more mutinous.

Ignoring their clamour, the Christina Noble side saw off Swansea and got past a French touring team in the semis. The final was before us and one last game on a big stage. Somehow, we managed to beat the charity side Wooden Spoon, before collapsing at the end.

In the main event, the Kiwis narrowly shaded an epic against Fiji. The fireworks exploded, the Kiwis obliged with the Haka, the crowd went wild. Sevens rugby at its best – a crazy time with a seriously tough backbone. Long may this most schizophrenic of sports continue.

Bulgarian bruises

It was in April 2007 when I got an odd request to play rugby in Bulgaria. The lure of the unknown and the chance to help a children's hospital got me dusting off my not-so-long-retired boots.

I began to question the wisdom of coming out of retirement at about the time I was hit in the ribs by the Bulgarian centre. It had all seemed like such a good idea when an old university friend had asked if I could help raise money for a children's hospice in Sofia.

The next thing I know, I am in the Balkans running a move with a team-mate who hasn't played rugby in 15 years and who later told me he was not wearing his contact lenses. This meant that while I headed across field and waited for him to cut back, he never arrived. I, however, was bundled to the ground, skinning my knees and twanging a hamstring. Sitting in the dust, I wondered what the hell I was doing there.

This was as far from professional rugby as you could get and a world away from the sport I left behind only last May. The weekend had started much the same as many other rugby tours. Packing my bags had brought with it the old excitement. I got the same nervous flutter as I polished my boots, rinsed the gum shield and dusted the blazer. At the airport it was the usual mix of best friends and new faces. Then we landed in Bulgaria and my preconceptions were blown away.

I knew next to nothing about the country other than that it was the European Union's newest member where the average wage was about £100 a month. I had no idea that Bulgaria was 92nd out of

95 in the IRB rankings, ahead only of Israel, Finland and Bosnia & Herzegovina. I did not know they had a national league and a healthy smattering of clubs. I certainly wasn't prepared for Sofia's new airport, glorious sunshine and a horizon of snow-packed mountains and beautiful architecture. Neither were most of the boys in the team, the curiously named Purple Nasties.

As we headed into Sofia the mood was uplifting and decidedly amateur. This was a trip where training would come five minutes before kick-off and we quickly fell into the true rugby stereotype. Jim Telfer was right when he said that British rugby people go abroad and find the nearest Irish bar. We looked at the inside of a church for 90 seconds and, our sense of culture satisfied, headed to Flanagans. Just as Jim also predicted, we enjoyed burger and chips before heading to Murphy's bar where we got the first glimpse of our opponents.

They do not breed them small in Bulgaria; remember, this country has always been tremendously strong in the world of weightlifting and wrestling. Our hosts in Bulgaria and main opposition in the charity tournament were Pernik, the 23-times national champions. Sitting around a long table at the back of the bar were most of their 1st XV.

You knew immediately that while they might not test you in the wide-open spaces, you would not want to find yourself anywhere near a dark maul. They had huge piles of meat on the table and vats of lager, and they all smoked. As we strode into the bar, eyes turned to see who was venturing on to their turf. Heads down we worked our way towards them, unsure of what reaction to expect. We needn't have worried, for once the rugby connection was made, it was as though we had been friends for life. Broad smiles, bear hugs and vice-like handshakes. Rugby was our common bond and they explained that they loved the game for the physical side of a sport that won them respect and impressed the local ladies.

The next morning we were up early and heading out of Sofia on a bumpy ride to the match pitch in Pernik, an industrial town on the outskirts of the capital. Enormous pipes and rubbish were everywhere, and among this decaying industrialisation we chanced upon the pitch. There was one uncovered stand, with concrete steps and seats, a changing room, a 1970s ambulance and an old lady selling nuts. There was a barbecue and a beer pump. Waiting for us were the Pernik squad whom we had agreed to train before the tournament. One translator and 50 giants would test anyone's coaching credibility but it was never anything other than an absolute joy. They lapped up tips on scrummaging and line-outs, putting them into practice with unexpected talent and ability.

As an old disciple of Phil Larder, I finished with a defensive session. I apologise to the boys from Wasps, but Pernik will drift and not blitz. They started quiet and shy. By the end of the defensive session they were pointing at empty space, shouting their heads off and, most worryingly, chasing me all over the shop.

By now the crowds had started to arrive, techno-dance music blaring out of speakers. In the car park, Ladas nestled beside Porsche Cayennes, some people clearly enjoying Bulgaria's new market economy more than others. The tournament was split into two groups. In the Purple Nasties' side of the draw were the national sports academy and Pernik B. In the other half with Pernik were the Moscow Dragons and the Sofia-based Murphy's Misfits. You realise what a small world it is when Jason Leonard has been a guest speaker at the Moscow club and Murphy's Misfits were fielding an Obolensky, a direct descendant from the one and only flying Prince.

The group games were concluded without mishap – unless you

include the Dragon who had four stitches put into a hole in his head that needed at least 20, done with what looked like a fish hook and a Swiss Army knife, and not an anaesthetic in sight. As the final between the Nasties and Pernik neared, the mood changed. The boys realised we were in for a tough match and that we had not come this far to lose. While the shirts may have been a little ill-fitting and our positions on the field a little haphazard, there was no mistaking the desire to do a job.

I have been in many huddles before and there is no better feeling. It is that feeling that had got me back on the pitch. I pretended to myself that it was to raise money for the One Life Bulgaria charity and their plan to renovate a children's hospital and build a new one. It was, but only to an extent. Part of me will always miss that sense of belonging to a team, of playing rugby with friends. That's what got me back on the pitch and what got me back on my feet after they knocked the stuffing out of me.

In the end we beat Pernik in a hard-fought match that left us all with souvenirs of our trip. And while the bruises will fade, my memory of Bulgaria will not. On a national level they may be miles away from rugby recognition, but far from the spotlight and in among the old towns there are thousands of Bulgarians who absolutely love our sport.

Trying to keep up with the light blues

I went to meet the Cambridge boat race crew in 2008 and learnt just how tough rowing can be. Forget the training and technique, this sport is all about having a desire to win.

Walk into Cambridge University's rowing base on the banks of the river Cam, and it is not the tradition that smacks you in the face.

The Goldie Boathouse has history, of that there is no doubt. The captain's room upstairs is painted the university's famous shade of light blue. There are ornate carved chairs, and oar blades hang on walls decorated with the names of all the rowers and coxes who have represented the university since the club's inception in 1829.

Everyone who has taken part in the annual race against their great, dark-blue rival Oxford is commemorated. But to be honest, I had expected this musty sense of the past. What drew me up short were the two words painted above each year's Boat Race crew. They read only won or lost. Stunning in their beauty, unsettling in their simplicity, and damning in their conclusion. No pictures of how close the race was, or of how much effort was put in.

All that matters, all the crews will ever be judged on, was whether they were winners or losers. Welcome to the strange and supremely harsh world of the rower. I had always been curious about what made rowers tick. I wanted to know what it was about a sport that looks so simple and so dull that makes people such as Sir Steve Redgrave push themselves until they collapse. Why sit on a rowing machine – those dreaded ergos – for hours on end, day after day, week after week, staring at a wall and not going anywhere? And why is it that, as the Cambridge v Oxford rugby and cricket matches drift into insignificance, drowned by professionalism, the Boat Race is still a global spectacle that attracts Olympic and world champions?

You can imagine that when I was given the chance to spend some time with the Cambridge crew little more than two months before the next Boat Race, I all but ran to the train station. Within minutes of arriving, my preconceptions were shattered. I met up in a bar with Dan O'Shaughnessy, 2008's president, or captain as we might call him. A Canadian who shakes hands like a grizzly, he comes straight from the glossy magazines. With him was Toby Garnett, a lad from Putney who looks uncannily like the actor Rhys Ifans and has the physique to match.

Supremely fit athletes they may be, but sitting there with a pint of lager in hand, a burger and chips ordered and *The Simpsons* on the telly, they don't look so tough. Thoughts of wowing them at their own sport swam through my mind. They are still paddling about the next morning when I get a rude awakening and a painful introduction into just what it takes to make it as a top oarsman.

Rebecca Dowbiggin is the cox who guided Cambridge to victory last year and is still in the seat for the coming race. She puts me through a 17-minute rowing machine session that is meant to replicate the 4¼-mile Boat Race course that runs from Putney to Mortlake. As I pull on the ergo's chain, trying to keep the fan going, hands slippery from sweat, Rebecca explains what she would expect in a race. She knows the course blindfolded. She knows expected currents, wind speeds, when to turn in, when to let the boat run. Her touch can make or break the race and she needs to be flawless.

On the ergo, it is clear my technique can be worked on. As cox, Rebecca must gently persuade her crew to give her more power, to speed up their strokes, to find rhythm, to ignore the fact that they can hardly breathe. She must maintain the crew's tempo, unity and focus no matter what. She is all smiles and laughter with me but you can just tell that if she needs to she can turn it on. I feign ignorance and smile politely. I do not want to see her dark side.

The rowers tell me that the further down the course you go, the dumber you get. As fatigue begins to get the better of you, it is here that her simple, rhythmical calls earn their corn. I explain that in rugby we used to call it the mum test – calls which are so simple that your mum could understand them. The idea gets instant approval from Dan.

At the end of the 17 minutes I am spent. Every part of me aches, my lungs are begging for air, my head spins. It is a ferocious test of my abilities. Boat Races are hard work both on and off the water. For 2008's Cambridge crews, the journey began with a time trial that looked to whittle down the 50 or so men with their hearts set on winning a rowing blue. Should you fancy having a crack, make sure you can row 2,000 metres in close to six minutes.

Over the subsequent months, this group is trimmed down through selection or injury until a core group are left competing for 16 seats in two boats. On the day of the Boat Race, eight will win a blue in the main event, another eight will race in the second Goldie boat. In a couple of weeks' time, Dan the president will name two provisional crews. Changes can happen, but the eights will begin to work on their own strategies and plans for the race. It is just as tough for the coxes, and Rebecca is again under pressure from two rivals.

Away from the water, and when most professional athletes would be having a kip or playing video games, Cambridge's oarsmen again push themselves in search of excellence. In this year's squad of 20 there are students of history and physics. My own particular favourite, though, is Tim Perkins, an Australian studying for a doctorate in molecular biology who is working on the genetics of infectious diseases. Would you get in a boat with him?

I had very little choice, and during the squad's afternoon session I find myself dressed in Lycra and practising starts in the seat behind Tom 'The Caveman' Ransley. He would fit right into the second row with Sebastien Chabal and I push my luck on several occasions battering him in the back as I am going forwards and he is going backwards. His kidneys are taking a pounding, and I cross my fingers, hoping he is in a forgiving mood. Rowing on an ergo is one thing – bobbing about on the water it is a different matter.

There are so many things to think about. I am less than three inches from the water but miss it with the blade. My strokes are short, then I go too deep and it nearly flips me out of the boat. I start rocking. But even with me making an idiot of myself, the pick-up from standing start to that feeling of flying down the river is thrilling. You suddenly realise why they spend so much time rowing – a mere 80,000 metres last weekend. It is because they must find a way to work as one.

My time in the boat is over, and with me gone, the crew make it seem effortless. I ask Dan how he knows when it's all going well and he says it feels as if you are on tracks like a train. As they glide past some swans, their strokes in perfect time, waves breaking at the bow of the boat, I get a brief feeling of what it must be like. All the time the cox is watching and tweaking, upping rates, asking for adjustments.

Physical and mental, rowing uses every muscle. It's all about the power-to-weight ratio – you can't be too heavy or the boat drops too deep in the water, and you can't be too light as you cannot generate enough force. Balance, finding the right combinations of engine-room men, of technique men, of speed men. Henry Pelly, an old Etonian with a glint in his eye, is only just over six foot and is far from massive. He tells me he has a big heart which helps him oxygenate, fight the lactic acid in his muscles and keep going. I think he and the others have a switch in their brains that lets them turn off the pain. How else would they keep going?

The crews get Mondays off. They only train once on Friday but every other day it's twice, once in the boathouse in Cambridge and once on the river at Ely in the afternoons. They often start and return in the dark, before more studying and an early night. The next day, it all begins again. There is no money, there are no endorsements. It means sacrifices and pain. But amid all this harsh training there is joy and laughter, and the simple beauty of doing something that you love.

There is the deep camaraderie that exists between men who trust each other and would give their last breath for the cause. There is the knowledge that if they work hard enough, then when they revisit the old boathouse they will find only one word written next to their names, and it will mark them out as winners for the rest of their lives.

Nature's playground

Rugby gives you a weekly buzz – running out on to the pitch gave me that jolt no matter what was at stake. After I retired I found I kept looking for that same electricity and briefly found it again in some extreme sports.

It was a glorious summer's day in the Alps, and I was standing on the edge of a 6,000-foot drop with a small Frenchwoman strapped to my back.

Ordinarily I wouldn't have minded, but she was very clear about what I needed to do and unless I did exactly as she said there was a good chance we would end up hurtling towards the distant valley floor.

Not for the first time, I asked myself how the hell I had ended up in this situation. The simple answer was that I was on holiday. The more complicated one includes my post-rugby search for a sporting buzz, the possible warning signs of an impending midlife crisis, and finally getting the chance to do all the activities that were denied a professional sportsman. So, instead of hitting the beach, the wife and I headed for the extreme sports playground that has grown up around Chamonix and the nearby Mont Blanc.

I presumed that the French town would be busy during the winter months and the rest of the time would only be full of serious climbers and eco-tourists. I could not have been more wrong. Surrounded by imposing yet impossibly beautiful mountains, the town was teeming with people – the young, the old, families, babies in papooses, kids on bikes. They were from all over the globe, and they all looked very normal. Very fit, but nothing too scary.

Where was the death-defying craziness I had heard about? My first evening was spent visiting a friend, Ashley, who now lives in the town, and talking over plans for the week with our guide, Eddie. I slept soundly, and then on the first day I took a gentle walk up Le Montenvers and traversed the Mer de Glace – a sea of ice. I found myself going to bed thinking that there wasn't too much to this mountain lark. The next day, suddenly, everything changed.

Fear was my new best friend and he had moved in for the week. After an early start, we took the Flégerè cable car up the mountain and got ready for a tandem parapente flight. A simple sport, it involves strapping on a parachute and jumping off the nearest hill.

My wife got a Frenchman as a pilot, while I got a five-foot-tall bundle of noise called Crystal. Tied together, the problem we faced was that when I stood up on my lanky legs, her feet didn't touch the ground. She clung to me like a little lady rucksack and called me the giraffe. I knew her as the monkey.

She told me to start running and keep running until she said stop. I realised she meant down the mountain and nearly started to cry. Reality was kicking in. I blew a kiss to the wife and ran for my life. The ground was a blur, my heart pumping, ears popping, then suddenly silence. I was flying. The view was stunning, the tranquillity all-consuming.

Half an hour later, the gentle bump of landing brought me out of my reverie, and when two minutes later my wife arrived we relived our time in the clouds, smiles as wide as a Cheshire cat's. I should come clean now – I am a coward, I always have been.

Adrenalin can keep to itself. I don't go looking for it and if I had my way, every holiday would be a nice quiet one at my favourite family place in Portugal. But you know what? By the end of that hair-raising experience, I was beginning to look forward to the next crazy challenge. It didn't matter what it was, I perversely loved it.

During mountain biking I gripped the brakes, refused to let go and thanked goodness for the padded cycling pants. Canyoning saw me jumping off 12-metre cliffs without so much as a second thought, and the only time I wet my pants was white-water rafting, when I was too lazy to take off my wetsuit.

I did get scared, but that was when I was climbing down a set of ladders strapped to the mountain with 1,000 metre drops on either side. But I got through it and managed to put from my mind thoughts of just how dangerous mountains can be.

One night I ate with a legend of Chamonix, Jean-Marie, and his family. Jean-Marie is a man who has broken his leg and cut off his own cast after three weeks so he could get back up the mountains. A former Foreign Legionnaire and a doctor, he cooked with the Roux brothers in the Sixties and has climbed and skied places that snakes and mountain goats would fall off.

Listening to his stories, I was struck how easily and without arrogance the people I had met talked of events that for me are verging on the crazy. It is almost as though their proximity to danger gives them an understanding of how precious and exciting life can be, but also of how insignificant they are in the face of nature's awesome power.

One afternoon, while the wife was getting some retail therapy, I donned my boots and waterproofs, dumped the hire car and started following a trail. Three hours later and at more than 2,200 metres, I was atop the Aiguillette des Posettes, sitting above the clouds and rain, wondering why I had not escaped to the Alps before. If I am honest, it was down to fear and a worry that I would not make it out in one piece.

The trouble is, that is exactly the same mix of emotions that made the week of mountain sports so special and will have me coming back for more. Who would have guessed that a self-confessed coward could have had so much fun in nature's playground?

On your bike, Lol

In 2010, I returned to Twickenham, but not in the way I would have expected. Lawrence Dallaglio was on a charity bike ride and I found that joining him would be almost as exhausting as playing rugby with him.

If I thought that memories of halcyon days at Twickenham would flood back as I entered headquarters for the first time on a bike, I was sorely wrong. And I mean sorely. While Lawrence Dallaglio led the way bellowing out 'Swing Low, Sweet Chariot', my lungs, which had been burning pretty much since we had left Maidstone 5½ hours earlier, demanded silence. There was also the matter of the throbbing pain from my backside.

All my mental and physical energy was being consumed just trying to keep pace with Lawrence, as it had been all day on this, the latest leg of his Cycle Slam in 2010, which aims to raise £1 million for Sport Relief and the Dallaglio Foundation.

Lawrence's goal is to cycle to all of the Six Nations stadiums, covering 1,740 miles in only 24 days. Having started in Rome, he has already reached Paris and on Friday he led 70 riders, including me, into Twickenham like the Pied Piper of London after a much-needed pie and chip butty at Richmond.

We were met by Prince Harry, who had warm words of praise and encouragement for Lawrence. And while I struggled to conjure up flashbacks of famous wins with England or memorable tries, I noticed that little had changed.

England and Ireland had already finished the captain's run. Keith the groundsman was there, marking the lines and the camera crews were testing out their equipment.

I was tempted to head for the gym to seek a much-needed ice bath, given the state my body was in after pedalling almost non-stop for 70 miles from our starting point in Maidstone.

I just don't know how Lawrence keeps going. I was still walking like John Wayne by kick-off on Saturday. A lack of preparation didn't help. The last bike I owned was a BMX when I was about 12, and 20 minutes on a cycle machine in the gym three weeks ago was about all I could count on.

On the Tuesday, I managed about 50 miles of the leg from Paris to Albert before I had to stop because Lawrence got lost and I had to catch the Eurostar back to London. But that made me even more determined to complete Friday's leg.

Like a typical rugby player, I didn't put much thought into my gear. I turned up wearing trainers when everyone else had cleats, and ended up having to wrap cling-film around my shoes to keep them dry.

Then there was the bike. Lawrence lent me his spare, which was a serious piece of kit. The problem for me was operating the gears. It had three main ones, which each had a further 10 gears. I was stuck in gears 21–30 for the first half of the leg on Friday until a professional cyclist called Tom Davies took pity and sorted me out.

The day was not without incident. En route, one of the guys bumped into a car and the driver jumped out and offered James Cracknell a fight in the car park of a nearby Tesco supermarket. Cracknell, being more of a Waitrose man, declined the offer and we rode off.

My lack of cleats also saved me from a collision at traffic lights when my brakes didn't react as quickly as I hoped, as I was able to stop myself by putting my feet up on the bars at the back of a van.

Throughout, Lawrence was in his element. He is having so much fun because he is the consummate professional. He is where he is happiest. He is in control, as he was on the rugby field. He is in great physical shape, just as he was on a rugby field, and he still loves a beer, as he did in his rugby days.

He is morphing rugby into cycling and just as he squeezed everything out of his rugby career, he is getting everything out of this amazing and daunting challenge.

In terms of achievements, will raising £1 million for charity equal or top winning a World Cup for England? I don't know for sure. But as we cycled together into Twickenham, Lawrence did tell me this was the greatest thing he had ever done. And that's a pretty big statement.

School of hard knocks

I have always believed that sport can change lives. It can empower even some of the UK's toughest young men and turn around their prospects. And that is just what we tried to do when we took rugby to London's East End with Sky's School of Hard Knocks.

Playing rugby drunk is not a good idea. You would have thought most people would get this fact. But not Paulius from Lithuania. A small, young man who once came to training with marks on his neck from where someone had tried to strangle him, Paulius was not worried.

For him, training hammered was a walk in the park compared to surviving on the streets. I should have seen it coming. His kit bag always contained a four-pack of beer, and he said he needed to drink to sleep.

But when you are dealing with 25 lads from London's East End, a booze problem is the least of your worries.

That's what makes the *School of Hard Knocks* 2010 such a challenge. After the success of the previous series, when we turned a bunch of troubled Welsh kids into a rugby team, we thought we would try to repeat the process in one of London's most unforgiving areas.

Where Wales was all about local lads, this time round we got youngsters from as far afield as Portugal, Eastern Europe and Africa. They had problems and issues that I can't even begin to address in this article.

Still, at the core of what we were doing was the belief that rugby could change lives. We had our work cut out. The group contained the serial unemployed, habitual offenders, drug users, the homeless and the very, very angry.

From the first day there were problems. We almost had a full-scale riot seconds after the end of training on day one. Two phones had gone missing. There were accusations everywhere, all the boys in a room.

One lad said his bag would be searched over his dead body. I have used that phrase in jest down the years. That day, I thought it would happen.

There were trips to the hospital. There were the usual claims of prowess on and off the pitch. There was lateness and there was excuses, swearing, drama and threats.

But then there were genuinely moving moments, such as when they met Mark Prince, father of the murdered young Queens Park Rangers footballer, Kiyan.

This is a man who has seen what the street and knives can do in all its horror. He has watched doctors open the chest of his son, massaging his heart with their hands as they tried to pump life back into his dying body.

He is someone who has walked the dark side, who spent the first few hours after his son's death collecting the names of the people who had done the deed.

He is a man who speaks openly of how he was ready to exact revenge, an eye for an eye, on the first person who opened the front door at the house of the people he blamed.

But he is also someone who found the power to turn away from this path of destruction and death. Helped in part by faith, in part by an understanding that he had other children to provide for, he made the right choice. We wanted our group to see the man that Mark had become.

We wanted them to understand that they always, no matter what happens, have a choice. So we took them to the Repton Boys Club, where he could teach them the discipline that is required to become a young boxer, passing on the knowledge he gleaned as a professional fighter.

In his 40s, still in incredible shape, Mark punished the lads with his boxing training. When he spoke, you could hear a pin drop. This was a man from their parts, someone who has suffered but who was on the path to redemption. And how this young group of men would have followed him, right there and then, if only the path had been a literal one. But life is never that easy.

Another day we tried to show them that the police, the men in uniform they hated so much, were also human. So we took them to Gravesend, to spend time at the Met Police's riot training centre.

At first the bricks and firebombs had the guys sprinting in every direction but forward, which is what the police have to do. Slowly the control and the discipline came, and they walked as one through flames and headlong into the hurled masonry.

It all helped turn them into a team, and it meant that they surprised us in the first warm-up match by actually winning it. Mikey in the centre was born to play at a higher level.

Derek at loosehead prop had never played rugby before, but did a passable impression of Gethin Jenkins. If only this kid had played some rugby as a youngster, we would have a star on our hands.

Kwesi, our temperamental wing, has the pace any self-respecting Premiership wing needs. There's a bit of aggro and arrogance about him as well.

He is a classic *School of Hard Knocks* kid – so much talent, articulate, good-looking but ultimately far too willing to take an easy option and blame life's cruel cards rather than graft for success.

You find yourself veering between wanting to kick him up the backside and give him a hug. Still, five tries in two games tells you all you need to know.

On the flank we had Rodall from the DRC, Democratic Republic of Congo, and I don't think I have come across a better athlete, in terms of endurance, on a rugby field.

He would turn up late, had limited English, no body fat and zero understanding of rugby. One session, I decided to put the team through an old England fitness test. It's tough, hitting the deck and sprinting, and lasts about eight minutes.

Rodall set off, and my jaw dropped. He came into the home turn 10 seconds ahead of any man I have known. Not happy to coast in, he flick-flacked the finish and landed perfectly with a smile and a Usain Bolt arm-raise. I couldn't speak.

When we told them they had to do it again because of a previous punishment, he repeated the feat. You could see the group growing in confidence.

After the first win, we set up a second match against Barking RFC, the home of Jason Leonard. They got a kicking but dug in, and we learnt more about them in that match than we had in the previous eight weeks. And so to the final game, against an invitation XV of mainly police officers at Eton Manor rugby club.

On the first day of the programme, I conducted a social experiment. I asked the guys to hug each other. They were embarrassed and did it quickly to get it over with.

Come game day, I asked them to repeat the process. I was overwhelmed. In that changing room there was genuine love and affection. Without exception, they were ready to do battle for each other. There was warmth, passion, friendship and tears.

United by this crazy sport, they had found many of the things that had been missing from their lives. They had overcome every hurdle, they had been hurt and laughed together, and they had become a team.

As they walked out on to the pitch, for the first time since I had met them, I could see that they felt like winners.

In the firing line

I was happily retired when I was asked back on to the pitch for the Help for Heroes game. Their bravery made it the easiest decision I have ever had to make.

There are certain calls you cannot refuse, no matter what promises have been made to the wife. For me, it all happened under the cover of darkness, a clandestine meeting at a restaurant, a load of red wine and chat.

On the other side of the table were Lawrence Dallaglio and his great mate, Steve Hayes, a director of Wasps and managing director of Wycombe Wanderers FC.

They had a proposal and it excited and frightened me at the same time – did I fancy a game of competitive rugby against some of the biggest names in the world game? My first instinct was to smile, shake hands and tell them to go find some other skinny centre who had spent the best part of two years sitting on his bum and having fun.

But, just as I was about to make my excuses, they told me what it was all about and I put any personal fear to one side and signed up immediately. This was no jolly, no ego massage for aging former internationals – this was about raising money for our armed forces, for the brave men and women who risk their lives every day and as a result have been injured in places such as Afghanistan and Iraq.

For most of my rugby life, the game was mainly about what I wanted to get from it, about my ambitions, my performance. With this charity match, to be played at Twickenham on September 20, and its aim of raising £1 million for 'Help for Heroes', I could perhaps make life easier for people who had never asked what was in it for them, but had simply done what their country needed.

So the deal was done, and I was officially out of retirement, again, and on the phone looking for a place to train. Harlequins came to my rescue, and after a gentle warm-up session with some seriously talented amateur players at Salcombe RC, I found myself back on the training pitch in west London.

And my oh my, how times have changed. The first thing that shocked me was the colour of the boots that the players now get to wear. Mine arrived from a kind sponsor, and I opened the box expecting to find the good old-fashioned black leather clod kickers.

No such luck – they were white.

I always hated blokes in white boots, but nowadays unless your footwear is all the colours of the rainbow then you are very much yesterday's man, so I am told.

The next thing you notice is the quality in the car park. Gone are the Maestros, Astras and Mondeos which used to carry players around, chugging and backfiring from one training pitch to the next. Instead there are brand-new and shiny Range Rovers, Mercedes and Lexuses.

On a positive note, I needn't have worried about standing out in my boots – it was like a Milan fashion shoot.

I am not sure what the old heads of Jason Leonard and Brian Moore would have made of it.

Training started – I had managed to dig out the shoulder pads and buy a boil-in-the-mug gum guard – and it was like my first day at school. I dropped the first ball, didn't catch the call, panicked and passed the next to no one.

The younger guys began to smell decay and fear. It was not

pretty. But then, slowly, things began to make more sense, I began to feel more at home.

Old calls like 'fade out', 'ice' and 'clock' were still being used, they had just become 'bounce out', 'fix it', and 'pinch'. The banter was still there. Forwards doing line-outs and scrums, backs practising attacking and defending from set pieces.

Any time a break was made or a try was scored, faces were noisily rubbed in their weaknesses. Hilarious to be reminded of exactly what Healey, Catt, Balshaw used to do and how there is no escape when you make an error.

In between sessions the players wolfed down boiled eggs, mackerel, sweet corn, coleslaw, fruit, cereal, piling in as though they were at The Ivy.

Then the meetings, as all minds begin to focus on the opening game of the season, against Saracens. If you want to say something make sure it's interesting or right – dull and wrong and you will be hounded out.

The coach announces the team for a warm-up game. Some superstars have arrived, some new academy lads get the nod. There are the older guys who are friends, who tell me I have lost so much weight that Jonah Lomu and Scott Gibbs won't even notice I am on the pitch.

Then out for the defence session. Hard work, lungs bursting, still keep telling myself not to make an idiot of myself. As new as it all seems, the old stuff is still there. The hard work, the respect, the disappointment, the joy, the team, the individual, the fun, running around on a weekday afternoon with a bunch of your mates pushing yourself physically and mentally.

Army friends tell me this is why the armed forces love rugby, and its unique mix of physical confrontation, endurance and teamwork. They also tell me that it is the only time, within organisations that are heavily disciplined and structured, that other ranks can batter the living daylights out of officers and NCOs while offering up the most vitriolic abuse – and all with complete impunity.

At Quins, with the training session over, we pile into an ice bath that is both gloriously refreshing and a chilling reminder that while we sit shivering, others are in places far hotter and more dangerous. And as different as our situations may be at this moment, rugby is the common bond that can bring fun and help in equal measure.

When you retire from international rugby, there is always a glimmer of deluded hope that you will be asked back. When that doesn't happen, you are grateful for any chance that comes your way to relive those experiences. Help for Heroes was such an opportunity.

A match to raise money for soldiers injured in Afghanistan and Iraq was never going to be taken lightly. Add to that a crowd of more than 50,000 and the fear of leaving Twickenham on a losing note, and the scene was set for a cracking game. As part of the England invitation XV, my pre-match nerves were as bad as I had ever had. Food was pushed around the plate, a sickness in my stomach.

The bus was like a time warp. In the middle of the back row was Mark Regan. Always the same spot for me: aisle seat, one row from the back on the left. Boys from the Armed Forces dotted around us, open-mouthed as Martin Johnson gets a going over, back to being one of the lads, and banter that's funny, harsh and fair.

In the changing room you see why Wasps will always miss Lawrence Dallaglio so much. Inspirational words, reminding us why we are there, of what it means for those watching and why we mustn't let anyone down. He calls on the armed forces to lead us out and Matt Cornish of the RAF, the ranking officer, steps to the front of the line. Colleagues from the Army, Navy, RAF and the

Marines are in behind him, pride swelling their chests, emotion wetting their eyes. Then we are out on the turf.

The national anthem starts up and we sing it loud and clear, old hands realising that it really is the last time; young players hoping it is the first of many occasions; the armed forces understanding the true cost of protecting Queen and country.

The game is quick and open from the start. I look at the opposition and worry about the size of their front five, but our young pack fights hard and wins us ball. Again I am amazed at the speed of the props, the ability of all players with the ball in hand, and how much the game has changed even in the short time since I left it. Multi-functional is the key today.

I see faces from yestercar, the likes of Scott Gibbs, Colin Charvis and Jonah Lomu, and I try to take it all in one last time. At the final whistle the powerful applause of the crowd takes me by surprise. But the cheers are not for the players – they are for the men and women standing side by side a long way from home, and they are sending a message that no matter what happens, we, the rugby community, will be there for them when they get home.

Rugby Can Teach You A Few Things

Rugby seems like a simple game. For a lot of critics, you pick up a ball and run into or around people and that is about it. But there is more to it than simple skills and contact. Rugby is about brains and emotions. It is about understanding yourself and your opponents and about rethinking plans and reworking expectations. This 'stupid' game has taught me some of life's most important lessons and, best of all, they have helped me keep working today.

When an opportunity comes along, grab it

Where is the other you right now? The you that made the tube, not the you that sprinted and arrived as the doors slammed shut. The you that went left and avoided the M25, not the you that is stuck at junction 15 in the world's largest car park.

We all do it, wondering what life would be like if we had made different decisions at key moments. Sport is no different. What would have happened in 2005 if Brett Lee had smashed Steve Harmison's full toss for four? Instead it was a single and he had to watch Michael Kasprowicz get out in the same over, losing the match and levelling the Ashes series. Would a million people have welcomed Steven Gerrard's Liverpool home with the European Cup if the referee had judged that Luis Garcia's goal had not in fact crossed the line against Chelsea in that pulsating semi-final? And, on a personal note, would I have ever won a Lions Test cap if Brian O'Driscoll had not gone into 'that' ruck?

The sporting commentator labels them 'what ifs', the unanswerable questions that prey on the mind of those who end up on the wrong side of those decisions. Such turning points can give victors the confidence to go on to great things, but only if they refuse to dwell on the fact that it could so easily have been different.

It is all down to twists of fate and split-second decisions that would have even the most hardened sadist wincing in sympathy. As harsh as it must seem, there is no point crying over what might have been. In sport, the imponderables are so numerous that to let them prey on the mind would drive an athlete insane. It is how we react to these twists of fate that determines greatness.

The cricket boys saw the opportunity they had to win the Ashes and snatched it with both hands. Liverpool showed their class by going 3-0 down in the final and still brought home the trophy. And O'Driscoll? He has bided his time and put in the groundwork. He has trained away from the big crowds and the flashing lights, and reappeared on the European stage last week in the most emphatic of ways, playing brilliantly.

Martin Johnson's boys of 2003 had their own moments, not least when, seconds from glory in normal time, Australian fly-half Elton Flatley stepped forward and converted a penalty that many claim should never have been given. Argue the point for as long as you want, it made no difference at the time, and we had no choice but to play on and send the whole nation behind the sofas for the last 20 minutes.

Forget about ifs, should haves or coulds. They are an irrelevance. It does not matter what the other you is up to. In sport when an opportunity comes along, grab it with everything you have, do not let go and enjoy the moment wherever it takes you. Fail to concentrate on the here and now, and there is a good chance that, come a cup final, the other you will be wondering about what might have been.

Think correctly under pressure

Sir Alex Ferguson and Sir Clive Woodward both have a thing for teacups. The context may differ, but the sporting gurus have employed them to similar effect.

Sir Alex prefers the physical object and the psychological shock that can be generated by throwing a very English object at his players, many of them from foreign shores. In Sir Alex's grasp the humble teacup turns into a motivational hand grenade that can have even the toughest defensive midfielder quaking in his boots. Ducking shrapnel leaves a player in no doubt that unless an attitude is changed or a finger pulled out then he too will be joining the long list of players who have failed at Manchester United's Theatre of Dreams.

Sir Clive was just as ruthless and while his TCUP, or Think Correctly Under Pressure, is more a state of mind, he would not hesitate to show the door to any player who did not measure up to what was required. Aren't our Olympians lucky to have him as director of elite performance at the British Olympic Association?

Show yourself to be capable and have the right mental strength, on and off the field, and it will be welcome to the club. Miss the point ever so slightly and it will be thanks for coming, as the gates to Fortress Twickenham and your international career clang shut behind you.

So what is TCUP? It is the ability to control aggression, to know when to push the referee, when to slow the ball down or have your prop fake an ankle injury. It is knowing when to take the points, play for territory or unleash the blitz. It is a catch-all phrase that sums up a player's ability to stay cool and do the right thing. In short, it is knowing how to win.

At the highest level, margins of victory are becoming smaller. In the first week of the Guinness Premiership in 2006, three games were decided by the margin of a penalty goal, while four of the six games were decided by less than a converted try. Wasps, London Irish and Northampton emerged victorious by margins of two points or fewer, Heineken Cup finals never have more than a score between the teams, World Cup finals are guaranteed to go to the wire and I was relegated two seasons ago by the width of a post. Teams who fail the TCUP test open the door on games they should have locked up and shut down.

At the start of a season defensive systems have been put in place and trust has been handed from one man to the next. To commit an illegal act at a ruck within kicking distance is a betrayal of trust, plain and simple.

Players can push a referee early on in a match, and any forwards coach worth his salt will ask his pack to see what they can get away with at rucks and mauls, because in the modern era slow ball is dead ball. But you do not test a referee with 78 minutes on the clock. And when you have to do it, you make sure it is in the right part of the field, well out of kicking range. Then it is not a hot-headed act that lets people down, it is rugby in the real world.

To win at the highest levels you must be able to think correctly under pressure. If you cannot, you let your team down and that, in team sport, is the ultimate faux pas. Sir Clive and Sir Alex may use them differently but essentially TCUPs and teacups have the same purpose – they let you find out who you want in your camp and who you are better off without.

Trust your team-mates

Clive Woodward had a way of building his teams up the night before games. His message was very simple, and was designed to have you feeling quick and strong. It would go something like this, I can almost hear him saying it now: 'I would not swap one of their players for one of ours. As I go down this team-sheet, I passionately believe that, man for man, we are better in every department. It is absolutely critical that you believe me when I say that not one of their players would get into our team.' Rousing stuff. It was done to make you feel confident and relaxed about your team-mates, and optimistic and bullish about the prospect of a glorious English victory. His message was always followed by some articulate, quiet pearls of wisdom from Martin Johnson. You would leave the meeting room wishing you could play the game right there and then.

And before your stomach could get too many butterflies, you were faced with feeding time at the zoo. Another smart move, the meeting wrapped up, you would head off to the restaurant to fill your belly with the usual Friday-night choice – Thai green chicken curry, lasagne, spaghetti bolognese and the treat we had all been waiting for, bread and butter pudding. This last dish never altered over four straight years. You don't mess with a rugby player's routine; they are creatures of habit. No bread and butter pudding, no smiles, no play. It's not the rugby I miss, it's the night before the games, the nervous anticipation, the tension, the pudding. So, there we were in October 1999, the group stages of the World Cup, on the eve of the New Zealand clash.

It was a must-win game because if we didn't top our group, we wouldn't win the cup. The lads assembled in the meeting room of the Petersham Hotel in Richmond. The flip chart was out, the teams were written down, we knew the drill, time to feel good about ourselves. Clive began: 'Jason Leonard, simply magnificent . . . Martin Johnson, the best ever . . . Dallaglio, in a league of his own . . . Guscott, simply magical . . . Perry, a rock upon which we build' – all good stuff. But, strangely, there were giggles from the back. Nothing was said and we moved on. It wasn't until dinner that we discovered the reason for the mirth. As the front-five forwards huddled together trying to work out what each piece of cutlery did, they explained that they would, in fact, swap Austin Healey for Jonah Lomu. In truth, looking back at it now, there was a damn sight more than one of us we would have swapped back then.

Maybe three of the England team would have kept their places. We were leagues behind the men in black. No matter, because by 2003 Clive had worked his magic, making us believe in ourselves. We found ourselves honestly believing that we would not have swapped one of our players for anyone else in the world. That takes some saying, but I know all my old team-mates would agree. A team like that is an amazing place to be. There is no feeling like it in the world; not arrogance, just total belief in one another.

Don't be blinded by science

Fermat's last theorem took mathematicians 357 years to prove. Not an easy subject, numbers. Not easy at all, and rugby players aren't feted for their grey matter. I have heard players order a Kofi Annan in Starbucks, and ask how someone got their birthmark. Our reputation for being a bit dense is sometimes deserved, though it often isn't. True, we get hammered around the head, but learning a dictionary of backs and line-out moves keeps you sharp. Also, you should never forget players like Jon Webb, who is a top orthopaedic surgeon, and others like Tim Stimpson with his love of Jean-Paul Sartre and all things French and existentialist.

Mention sums and normally level-headed coaches start totting up possible points and bonus scores, working out what they need and what their rivals have to do, and then tailoring their game plans to fit the equation. They may as well think of a number between one and 10, times it by five, divide it by their wife's age, and then roll it up and stick it in their ear.

You think I am exaggerating? Look back to Wasps and the 2004-05 season. The defending champions went into the last game thinking they needed to win with a bonus point against Biarritz if they wanted to qualify. They turned down penalty after penalty going after those damned elusive tries, only to lose 15-18 and find out when it was all too late that a simple four-point win would have been sufficient. As if that wasn't bad enough, their innumeracy meant that their old enemy Leicester did qualify for the later stages. I don't care what you say, that bad taste would still be in my mouth years later, no matter how many beers I sank.

Still need convincing? Then come further back in time with me to 1996 and Maine Road, the then home of Manchester City, a team that has taken number dyslexia to PhD levels. Alan Ball was the manager and we were in a relegation battle, playing Liverpool at home in the final game of the season. The score was 2-2, when Ball heard a rumour from the crowd that Southampton, our rivals for the drop, were losing to Leeds. That meant a draw would be enough for City to stay up and Steve Lomas was ordered to head for the corner flag and kill time. Genius. Or it would have been if the rumour hadn't been false and Southampton weren't also drawing, enough for them to stay up.

My lasting memory of that game was of Niall Quinn, who knew the real situation, sprinting up the touchline in a desperate attempt to tell Lomas to stop messing about and get the ball into the penalty area. The truth came too late, City ran out of time, were relegated on goal difference and left to rue what might have been.

Teams cannot allow themselves to be blinded by science. They have to concentrate on winning, on building a score, on forcing their rivals to play from deep. Only when the game is well and truly won can they even think about playing sevens rugby, hunting extra points and trying to split the atom. Concentrate on the basics of winning rugby and play your own game. Then if you don't make it through, you can at least say you have given it your best shot.

Forget the maths and try not to think about it too much because, as any rugby player will tell you, that is the quickest way to a very painful headache that will take a whole year to shift.

Prepare with rituals

The week before a Test match is all about removing luck, about controlling what is controllable, about ensuring 22 players are in the best possible state to play their optimum rugby.

Selection has already been made, training has been planned and is completed. Media day is fulfilled. Tactics are discussed, downtime is enjoyed with a day off, while the final team run took place yesterday, so that i's could be dotted and t's crossed.

The night before the game a film will have been watched, a massage enjoyed, a final supper devoured. Sleeping tablets get swallowed by some, hot chocolate for others. Come match day and lunch is pushed around the plate, because the butterflies will allow nothing else. After what seems like an age, bags are loaded on to the bus and the journey begins. Music is listened to, cars are overtaken with the help of a police escort, arrival planned for 90 minutes before kick-off.

Players collect their bags and walk through the crowds to the changing room. You hear the noise but retreat into your own world. Kickers get changed early, always the first out. The front row find a dark corner, staying close, aware that, come game time, they must go to a place where none of us can follow.

Physios and doctors are flat out, as most players will have ankles and shoulders strapped. Some are lucky enough to require neither, others resemble Egyptian mummies. Many players will read the programme, others clean boots, change studs so that some are longer than others. Lucky socks get worn, right boots on before left. The soundtrack is provided by iPods playing the theme to *Rocky*, Take That, the Clash, whatever gets you on the edge.

More and more players drift out on to the field, differing routines for different positions. Some jog around the field nice and slow, heart rate beginning to creep upwards, others are out of the blocks, spinning, stepping, accelerating. Then the rush of adrenalin that follows with the knowledge of what is about to take place. Refocus. Half an hour to go, back into the changing room. Team uniform for warm-up, match shirts put on only closer to the time. Many hit the caffeine trying to perk up and boost awareness levels. It's legal. Others stay on the water.

Time for a sit-down, the coaches take centre stage. A talk through, the opening kick-off routine reminded. Defence coach reiterates the importance of solidity. Attack coach talks of patience, discipline. The head coach gives a final overview, underlining opportunities that have been gone over all week, reminding the side of their basics, of their structure, of their game plan. Then they have finished.

Team huddle as the captain has a quick word, trying to hold his troops back. The fitness guru is waiting outside, so the captain leads his boys out and the crowd react. Players are in the zone, but not all. Some have not yet flicked the switch. Each to their own. Warm-up. Heart rate raised, really raised. You had better be ready. A split – forwards and backs go their different ways. Forwards must do more line-outs, must hit something and preferably each other. Bone on bone tells them it is almost time. Backs enjoy the feel of the ball hitting their hands, of delivering the perfect pass.

A move is rehearsed. Then the squad come together again. Team-play, half a pitch covered, patterns rehearsed. Hit a power runner, zip it wide, focus on the coach's key points, the fly-half and scrum-half beginning to take control. Some rucking drills, some power running and then some hits. This is not training-ground stuff. Bags are hit at full tilt, replacements bellowing encouragement.

The sweat is pouring off you; you wonder how you will manage a game – and then it ends. A last word on the field and a walk back to the changing room. Water bottles gulped on. The intensity of the occasion has your blood pumping. Shoulder pads on and helmets secured. Shirts fitted into – the new ones are so tight you may as well paint them on. Physios, kit-men, replacements all help. Boots are re-tied, gum shield kept in hand or shoved down sock. The five-minute knock on the door from the ref.

At that moment you could be English or Scottish, French or Italian, Welsh or Irish. You could be at Twickenham, at Cardiff, at Rome. No matter what language you speak, when the knock comes you must be ready for confrontation, physical and mental. You must be ready for punishment. You have to be ready to go to work. It is here that the game is decided. This very moment. Not in the anthems, not the first kick, not the first points. It happens in the changing room, with your mates.

Your rugby soul stripped bare, the reason you play the game. A final handshake, a final hug, the captain's final words. Looking around a circle of faces and seeing the unity, the desire. It is then that you know the game is won, that the game is yours.

Win ugly

Bob Dwyer is a hell of a man. World Cup-winning coach, Australian to his core. He said what he liked and he liked what he said.

Dwyer had a turn of phrase like no other. When you ran with the ball he implored you to move 'as if a tiger was chasing you. No!

A man with a knife'. But best of all was his description of how he wanted you to react when the ball went loose during a match. Bob would scream at you to fall on it as if it were a bomb and your family were in the room. 'Smother the bloody thing quickly,' he would shout.

In today's game much is made of keeping the ball in your hands, of running and offloading. But ignore the dirty work on the floor at your peril. Where it was once the realm of the No 7, who prided himself on the art of killing and nicking the ball, today it is the job of every player from 1 to 15.

This battle for 50/50 possession – a mix of honest Corinthian spirit, a determination to win and great technique – can swing a game.

The set-piece scrums and line-outs have retained their value. However, win the breakdown, snaffle loose ball, and a team can neutralise this threat. Don't knock on, keep the ball in the tackle, run straight, recycle rigorously and viciously, and why do you need to go to set pieces? Space will appear, gaps come if you are patient and hungry.

Now I don't want to make out that there's no technique involved in winning the battle on the floor. It takes hard, painful graft to get it right. On the 1997 Lions tour, Jim Telfer had a stick he used to whack you with if your body position was too high as you practised rucking drills. He didn't just tap you either, especially when you were a six-foot five-inch public school three-quarter who had always thought rucking was something only forwards did.

When he was England forwards coach, John Mitchell was a nasty man in this area as well. His hard Kiwi edge came through. John used to get four players inside a three x three-metre grid that had long tackle pads for their sides. Men with tackle shields and tackle suits would stand over the pads wanting to cause you as much pain as possible.

The drill was simple and it lasted a minute. The scrum-half put the ball in front of a pad and you had to ruck the men away from it, then you moved on to the next pad. But make any mistake, put a loose foot on the ball, commit an offence by losing your feet and it meant you went back to the start. The more tired you got, the more mistakes you made.

John would shout at us to 'let the dog see the rabbit'. I think I understood what he meant. Huge bodies were flying and it was chaos. Pad to pad, body position ever lower, aggression increasing rather than diminishing.

In 2005, Eddie O'Sullivan had a net placed over the rucking area in the old Commonwealth Stadium in Christchurch and the Lions midweek team went about whacking lumps out of each other at almost knee height.

The Argentinians in the World Cup were frenzied at the breakdown, while teams such as Munster have been creating havoc for years. For the All Blacks, the loose ball and rucking are almost a rite of passage. Bravery is needed – it is a dangerous place to be.

Players have to commit and they have to do so 100 per cent, regardless of who they're playing for, be it Leicester at Welford Road or the local school pitch. Unless that happens there will always be a man on the other team who will want it more.

A pack of hungry scavengers do not need much knowledge about the intricacies of rugby. They don't have to be able to pass off their left hand or have a turn of speed or a scything sidestep. All they need is to boss the breakdown and eat the scraps. This will rebalance power from the fancy player to the ugly player. It is why our game is so beautiful – people with no airs or graces can be almost impossible to beat because they do not mind having their nose rearranged for the seemingly thankless task of re-gathering a loose ball.

Don't pile errors on top of errors

As a man with three kids I spend a lot of time watching young people melt down. You can see it happening. A mixture of excitement, emotional fatigue and too much information often causes a complete collapse of the central nervous system. One minute they are having fun and messing about, the next they have brought Tesco to a halt, screaming blue murder and begging complete strangers to save them from their terrible parents.

So, bearing in mind that there is a little bit of the child in all sportspeople, should we really be surprised when the professionals suddenly have their own toddler moments, the walls of their expensively built, game-playing psyche crumbling around their reddening ears? And isn't it compelling when it happens?

For me, the fascinating thing in sport is not the reaction to the great moments. Rather it is how the individual or team deal with the smallest errors, the sudden lapses of concentration, the onset of fatigue and subsequent tricks the tiredness can play on both body and mind.

When Rory McIlroy hit his golf ball into the log cabins on the 10th hole at the US Masters it began a chain of events that defined a tournament. The drive was recoverable.

In fact, Rory had a relatively nice approach to the 10th green when he hacked out and a five would not have been the end of the world. These things happen, the pressure can tell after leading for 63 holes. Even the fact that he finished with a seven on that hole wasn't terrible. What finished him off was the 12th.

When he four-putted on the par three you could tell he had

gone in his head, the thought processes abandoned, the brain switched off for a few moments. The crack had appeared on the earlier hole, and it looked like he couldn't put it behind him and move on.

He has not been alone. Paul Scholes is a genius footballer but he has his moments. When he got sent off against Manchester City at Wembley it was down to his poor first touch.

There was very little danger, but his reaction to his inaccuracy caused the red card. Instead of closing the ball down, working hard to correct an error that probably annoyed him and wound him up, he compounded the problem by putting in a knee-high tackle on Pablo Zabaleta that ended Manchester United's chances of a victory.

Sport, and especially rugby, is not just about actions, be they good or bad. It is all about the reactions. Control those and teams and individuals will flourish.

Take this incident from the 2011 Heineken Cup quarter-final in Dublin. Off the top of a line-out Leinster headed wide, and Brian O'Driscoll used some decoy runners in front of him to try to slide wide.

Anthony Allen, of Leicester, spotted this, and jumped in for a tackle he had to make (the simple rule is that if you jump in then you have to make the hit, no excuses). He missed and BOD was now on an arc round the corner heading for the open spaces. Tuilagi still had his winger outside him and his full-back tucked in behind, so while Leinster were on the attack, all was not lost.

Tuilagi must also have known that his inside covers were scrambling like fighter pilots to get across and help him out. What the young player needed to do was relax, stay calm, buy time, hang on and wait for other defenders to arrive while shepherding BOD towards the touchline.

What he must not do, and which was exactly what he did,

was compound the problem by going off on a one-man blitz. All the power was with the ball carrier and Tuilagi was picked off with ease.

Here is another example of what I am talking about. Newcastle were playing Leeds in April 2011 and were leading 20-7 as the half-time whistle approached. Newcastle were defending as a team, fighting for their Premiership survival. Leeds were attacking, searching for a win they hoped would ease their own relegation fears.

It was powerful stuff. Leeds threw everything at Newcastle but the Falcons held out, won a penalty, and it seemed as if the half was over. The ball just needed to be booted into touch.

Jeremy Manning, a source of offensive strength for Newcastle, picked up the ball as his forwards were drawing breath and congratulating themselves on surviving the Leeds onslaught. Manning then tapped the ball and booted it upfield . . . Newcastle have struggled to score from five yards out, never mind 95. Suddenly all hands were on deck, panic was everywhere, and moments later Leeds scored a converted try. From nowhere, the score was 20-14 at half-time. Leeds went on to win the game and sent Newcastle bottom of the league. A player or team must try not to pile error upon error. Only when they learn to do that can they have a serious chance of winning the big games and tournaments.

Become the referee's best friend

Ever wonder what your life would be like if it got the Hollywood treatment? I do, and I have spent hours trying to work out which blockbuster names would play my family, friends – and team-mates from 2003. Clearly Jonny Wilkinson would be played by Brad Pitt; Martin Johnson would be a young Kirk Douglas standing on a box; Lawrence Dallaglio would want to play himself because you just know he wants to be the next Vinnie Jones; Phil Vickery would be Robbie Coltrane; and Jason Robinson has to be played by Cuba Gooding Jr.

But for me, the best fit is Jack Black as Jason Leonard, an unlikely hero who rode to the rescue when his team needed him the most.

It was the final scene of 2003 when he got the call from the director, the Gene Hackman-esque Clive Woodward. Extra time is looming and the Australians are playing against the bad guys. Helped by the referee, the 'Darth Vader' Andre Watson, who has taken a dislike to the England scrum, they are starting to take control. There were no great speeches, a simple 'you are on' was all that was needed to get our hero into action. Leonard tossed his tracksuit aside and muttered 'about time'. The comment probably finished his England career on the spot but, like all great stars, he knew the next 20 minutes would be his moment to shine.

Jason/Jack trots on, and instead of going to his team-mates, he seeks out the Dark Lord Watson, and delivers a monologue that deserved an Oscar. 'Hello Andre, I believe there have been a few problems in the scrum as such [Jason always says 'as such' when he is serious].

'You know me, I won't go up, I won't go down. I will only go forwards or backwards. If you don't even want me to push, I won't, but let's sort this mess out. I won't concede any pens and if there are any problems you come and talk to your old pal Jase.'

And in that second the problems of the scrum disappeared, Darth decided the scrum could use the force, and Brad and Kirk could have their moment. The game-changing move wasn't a tackle, it wasn't a kick, a try or a line-out. It was a simple bit of communication that let the referee know he had a player on the field who was willing to listen, willing to play by his rules and willing to adapt.

That is what rugby is about. There are some rules that are obvious and easy to understand, but there are also some that need interpretation. Before the current World Cup, referees were told to focus on the breakdown, and were told how to run it. There was nothing sly about this. It was done in an open and clear way. It had a massive neon sign over it that said remember the back-foot law for offside, the side entry by both attackers and defenders, the need for the defender to release the attacker before going back in to snaffle a turnover or slow the ball down and only if on your feet. Get it wrong and the refs are going to hurt you.

What you can't do is ignore the ref because the ref is always right. For 80 minutes his interpretation is the only one that counts.

All international teams have to think about how to play the ref because every one is different. Before big games, the coaching staff of each team and the referee meet up to discuss what is required. In that meeting three players should be nominated as the ones who can approach the ref during the match to find out what tweaks and changes are needed. At the same time, players should be talking to each other all the time.

When the ref shouts 'hands off', a scrum-half should be

screaming the signal to his pack so they can stop competing and realign for the next defensive phase. You can't hear much at the bottom of a ruck, so you need help and simple calls.

We used the call 'dead'. It was a harsh word that got through the other noise. When you heard it, hands would shoot into the air like a kindergarten schoolroom, the players keen to show the ref they were nowhere near the ball.

No team can afford to alienate a referee. They have to remember that it is usually three things that change the course of a rugby match – the weather, injuries and the referee.

Defend without tackling

My dad knocked me out in 1990. At a caravan park in Cumbria. I was asking for it and that afternoon I learnt everything I ever needed to know about rugby. He got me with a swinging left arm. I never saw it coming; never stood a chance.

Please don't start ringing up Social Services; we laugh about it every Christmas. Northerners do things differently. It was one of the best lessons because learning to defend when you are outnumbered is one of the game's great arts. You need to learn not to panic, to trust the touchline.

You have to buy time for your inside men, players who seem miles away in the rush of a game, but who in reality can be with you in seconds.

You have to relax. That is what the great defenders do. Back in the summer of 1990, relaxing was the last thing on my mind.

The point of the drill was for my 48-year-old dad to stop four 17-year-olds from scoring. We had the ball and were 50 yards out. The one and only rule was that you could not cut back inside because if you did, then the imaginary inside cover would have you.

The exercise was meant to show that one man with the right angles and a good starting position can control space and time and disarm four bustling, hormone-driven teenagers.

He could, apparently, turn an inevitable try into rubbish. He could make the crowd, again imaginary but no less real because of it, curse us long into the night for blowing their celebrations and wasting a scoring chance. In the end it was frustrating. Dad kept bumping us into touch before we had reached the 22 never mind the tryline.

After a while, I'd had enough. It was time to show him who was boss, so I decided to step inside and score under the posts. He was not a genius of his time for nothing, nor was he an England back-row forward for free. He had the nasties needed and as I found out, he still had them up his sleeve. As I stepped in, his left arm swung.

I woke up to the reminder: 'I told you not to step inside!' Lesson learnt.

Now, I am not telling you this for sympathy. During the first weekend of the Heineken Cup 2011-12 teams were coughing up points because they were not making the right call in defence. I am not talking about when they ran the drift or blitz, rather when they were scrambling.

This happens when teams are under the cosh, when the opposition have got in behind them, have recycled quickly and have them on the back foot.

It is the time when our friends on the wing, the players we generally know as space cadets, have the tough decisions to make.

The key is to keep your options open. Not to commit. Let me give you some examples of what to do and what not to do.

Toulon versus Ospreys; the score is 14-12 to the Ospreys in France. A memorable win is on the cards, the minutes are running down.

Jonny Wilkinson of Toulon finds himself with the ball on the left side of the field, he gives a pass and receives it back, he is jinking across the field, looking for a weakness. The Ospreys' defence have men, there should be no panic.

All they have to do is shepherd him across the pitch, pick off the runners, everything is hunky-dory boyo. Toulon are on the front foot so it is vital that the Osprey players do not jump out of their defensive line. Keep together, keep working, and remember the touchline is your friend.

Then suddenly Nikki Walker loses the plot. Walker is out on his left wing, Wilkinson is heading towards it. Stay calm, Nikki, don't panic. But he cannot help himself and he runs in towards Wilkinson, not trusting his inside cover.

Walker's outside foot is facing in, his buttocks are now facing the touchline, he is in the wrong position and Wilkinson knows it. The ball is floated out to Paul Sackey in space, he races on to it and scores. Game over. A match that had been all but won by the Ospreys was given away by a man not trusting the team-mates on the inside.

The second example involved David Strettle, the Saracens wing, who scored a try against Clermont in the opening weekend of the 2011-12 Heineken Cup.

But he could have done better when he did not have the ball. Clermont went up the right and got in behind Saracens. They recycled quickly, and the ball headed left.

Strettle was on the right wing and knew he was in trouble and screamed for Ernst Joubert, a brilliant rugby player, to come wider. When that did not happen, he had two options.

He could either tuck himself in tighter to Joubert, just in behind him, and work with his forward, reassure him verbally and physically that he would not leave him hanging. His second option was to stay out wide screaming and when Joubert did not move, panic, jump in, hit nobody with an attempted tackle and concede a try.

I am sure that by now you can guess that he took option two when there was no need to panic.

I say again, in a loud Dick Greenwood voice: 'You always have more time than you think.'

Do not tell me times have changed, that is rubbish. Scramble defence is the same now as it was 40 years ago, and it will be the same 40 years in the future. How you react to what is happening in front of you in the blink of an eye will be no different.

Wingers can score brilliant tries, and for that we applaud them. Yet, more often than not, it is the wingers who can defend and stay calm and keep out tries that I would want in my side. The perfect example of how to do it came in the same opening weekend from Topsy Ojo against Munster when the Irish side were counter-attacking.

Johne Murphy of Munster was on the ball with Denis Hurley, the quick, big, left wing outside him. Ojo was in a 15-metre channel with cover inside him. He stayed behind his inside tackler, his inside foot was forward, his buttocks faced infield. He was in control. He stayed inside Hurley so the winger was trapped between him and the touchline. And then, beautifully, he let Murphy run.

The key is knowing that while Murphy may be moving, he is also going nowhere. The inside man, the inside defender is there, you trust him, so you wait, wait, wait. Murphy realises the alley is closing down, he is running out of space, and he has to make a decision. He blinks first, and passes to Hurley. Ojo, the string puller, the patient one, the man with the guts to wait, gets an interception, scores a try and wins the match.

The thing to remember is that there is no perfect science to it. It's a feeling, a fluid movement in the competing tides of attack and defence. You have to fight the urge to jump out and make the big hit. You have to be more coward than hero.

In the end, by doing nothing other than positioning yourself well and talking well, you can bring the most dangerous attacks to a juddering halt. Players can prevent tries without making tackles and in a contact sport that is a freaky notion.

But the best part of it all, is that there is no need to panic because as odd as it may seem once you understand the concept there is always plenty of time to get it right.

Chuck the kitchen sink at them

To drift or not to drift. That is a big question. So big, in fact, that the debate is raging in clubhouses across the land, and all the way to the door of the national team. Defence wins games, and how a team protects their line is a very personal thing. The old-school approach of drift is under attack from a brash newcomer, the pumped-up blitz, and no one is quite sure of the best way forward. But before I get too far ahead, let's look closely at both systems.

The drifters – like Leicester, Newcastle, and England – aim to push the opposition towards the touchline. They look to stay on the inside shoulders of the attackers, watch the moves unfold in front of them, advance at a pace dictated by the player on their inside shoulder, and when the numbers of attackers and defenders are equal go forward and make the hit. The term in international rugby is 'reactive' – let's see what they do, then snuff it out. It is also conservative, and not very destructive. But it has won the World Cup, and is very effective when put into practice by players with pace and brains – people like Jeremy Guscott, Allan Bateman, and Brian O'Driscoll.

The other camp, the non-drifters or blitzers, will scream 'Bah, humbug! Boring!' and demand to be let off their leash to go and smash someone.

These defenders will stand opposite, if not outside their men, rush up in channels with the outside men leading the line. They don't care what move is going on, they froth at the mouth and want to force their attackers backwards and inwards towards the heavy forwards who are waiting, gleefully, for any stray jinking wing three-quarters. This is what is called proactive defence – the 'get them before they get us' mentality. It is highly destructive in the most chaotic sense, and has won a European Cup, Tri-Nations and a Celtic League. It's great exponents are players such as Josh Lewsey, Sonny Parker and anyone South African.

The two systems have strengths, and they have weaknesses. Choose the drift and you are likely to be accused – as England were for many years – of giving away too many scores out wide. Take on the blitz and get it slightly wrong, and holes appear like in a Swiss cheese. I know what I am talking about because it happened to us at Harlequins. We dumped the drift in favour of the blitz in 2010-11 on a short-term trial and got hammered. Our team weren't set up for the blitz, and didn't have the players suited to put that sort of defence into practice. And it is all about practice.

Not too long ago, a team's defensive work was limited to a game of touch in the warm-up. No one wanted to spend time without the ball in their hands because why would you work all day, catch a train or drive to training, turn out on a black pitch in the rain and spend more than an hour working out what you would do when you didn't have the ball? No, it was far more important to concentrate on having some fun, concocting moves with a high difficulty tariff in the vain hope that once every three months you might just pull one off. If the opposition scored four tries then you would just have to score five.

Unfortunately, some genius realised that you spend roughly half the game without the ball and we witnessed the birth of the defensive coach. At first they were poached from rugby league, but today many of those breaking into the top ranks are from a union background. And as that changes, so it seems as if the game is moving away from drifters as the kitchen-sink chuckers take the game to new levels of physicality, hunting in packs, damaging the side with the ball.

Beware, however, the footballer, the thinker. There are ways through the middle of this seemingly smothering defence. The late-arriving player on a lazy run and line can cause havoc. There are huge gaps if a team member does not buy into the system 100 per cent or finds himself going backwards as the rest of his team-mates go forward, and a side who are not afraid to push the corners by putting boot on ball can find easy yardage in the territorial battle.

PART TWO

The Development
Of The Game

Rugby today is not the game I first started playing. When I pulled on my boots as a child, it was more about friendship than science. Over the last 30 years it has gone from being a way of life and a mentality to becoming a full-time profession. Boot money has been replaced by proper wages and the stars of the game can rightly consider themselves to be the equal of any professionals in any sport. I recognise the game of the past, but also realise that rugby can never return to where it was before. This is not such a bad thing in many ways. The cold war between union and league has thawed and there has been a sharing of talent and knowledge that has benefited both sides. At the same time, this increasingly global game has brought new players to the shores of the UK, enriching the domestic leagues and showing just how many different ways there are to score points, make breaks and ask if the referee is an idiot. It's not all good news, however, and rugby is now competing with all the other business sports to sign the best and genetically most able athletes. And with greater riches on offer so the demands on the young players increase. For many, rugby will be a job that will break their hearts. Even so, despite all the changes and challenges, I have never been more optimistic about the future and look forward to watching from the sidelines as the game keeps changing.

The Debates

Lessons from the past

It was only when I realised the difference between epithet and epitaph that I realised I wasn't being buried on Thursday. I was in fact receiving an honorary doctorate in civil law at my old university, the incomparable Durham. I am sure I will never hear such kind words again, unless listening from the other side.

However, I must question Professor David Fuller's comparison of myself to the ballet-dancing great, former chancellor Dame Margot Fonteyn. In his speech David suggested that our intelligence and creativity had simply manifested themselves in different forms. I should be so lucky. Bill Bryson, the acclaimed author, is now the chancellor and his speech talking of 19th-century vergers swinging from the rafters of Durham cathedral certainly made a pleasant break from the usual changing-room banter.

The occasion was tremendously humbling, especially when I realised that the accolade had previously been awarded to Prince Charles, the late Mo Mowlam, and the genius that was Charlie Chaplin. I was made to feel very ordinary and lucky indeed. The whole occasion was a magical one, not least being robed in a cloister that doubles as Professor McGonagall's classroom in the Harry Potter films.

It was as I visited many of my old haunts that I realised what an extraordinary role Durham University had played in allowing me to reach the highest levels of the game. As my train click-clacked its way up North, I had a funny feeling of going back in time, as though I would enter a tunnel and come out the other side as an 18-year-old on his first day as a fresher. Taller than I was strong, straight out of school, in 1991 I wasn't sure quite what to expect but it surpassed even my wildest expectations.

The first surprise was the standard of rugby. Now this was in the days before professionalism, when university sides often played the role that Premiership sides do today, spotting and developing talent. Players who had worn the Durham centre jersey before me included Will Carling and Phil de Glanville, and I lined up in the same team as Tim Stimpson, Duncan Hodge and a number who played for England Students and Under-21s. There even was Daniel Sibson, possibly the best second-row forward I ever played with who did not win a cap. The schedule was simple: two matches per week, two training sessions and relaxation aplenty. On Wednesdays we took on other universities, while Saturdays were reserved for local sides.

The quality varied, but all games had a point, a purpose. Against the other students we had a chance to play hard and fast, test ourselves against the best out there. We came up against household names and top players such as Kyran Bracken, Robert Howley and Richard Hill. When we went into the community, against teams such as Percy Park, West Hartlepool and Blaydon, we learnt to look after ourselves, to survive against 15 men who wanted to bash us simply for being students and then buy the first round of beers with a smile and a pat on the back. I was getting even more of the street smarts by travelling to play for Waterloo, trying to get as many matches under my belt as possible, learning my trade.

The games were intense and the friendships were lasting. I can still picture my agent and great friend, Nick Keller, in tears on a pitch in Wales after we won at Cardiff against the odds. Now he is a hard man, a No 7 known as 'the Ferret', someone who would bleed for his team, and yet it meant so much to win for his friends that he couldn't keep it all in.

I still get wobbly thinking about the massive party that followed us getting into the university cup final. To this day, I fret about why we lost key games. And I try to keep in contact with people such as Ted Wood, people who have dedicated their lives to university rugby. But as I pulled into Durham station not having undergone a miraculous rejuvenation, I realised that time and the game waits for no man. The place to play now as an ambitious young buck is an academy.

Signed up from an early age, today's youth teams are professionalism personified. The players are subject to the same rules as the top players, mix with the old pros, learn from them, and understand that what they do is a job. Winning and the importance of getting points is drummed into them, and they are very good from a much earlier age. They concentrate on what they are doing, often giving up further education to focus on their rugby careers.

While universities still put out strong sides, they are often missing the brightest young talent. The University Match is perhaps the biggest example of such a change, as Oxford and Cambridge are no longer packed with past and future internationals.

I have no problem with the modern game of rugby. It's just that I worry many young players may be missing out on a fuller life. A very small percentage of people ever get the chance to play at the very top, and it can often come down to luck and being in the right place at the right time. Some of the academy boys won't make it and will spend a lot of time sitting around, warming benches and kicking their heels.

As I enjoyed a pint at the Durham University rugby club's second home, the Dun Cow Inn, waiting for my train home, I thought, 'wouldn't it be a shame if they forgot to enjoy themselves and backed only the one horse'. Often it's not reaching the destination that matters, but the route you take to get there.

Codes in union

It used to be a them or us situation. You were either league or union and if you crossed the line it could cost you your career. Today, union borrows heavily from league using defensive lines and attacking ploys. But you can't ignore the fact that rugby is rugby no matter whose rules you play by.

I am not a gambling man, but sometimes fate throws up something so bizarre that you have to take notice.

An outing took me to the Royal Windsor races on Monday. I had to leave early, but not before I noticed that there was a nag in the 5.20 with my name, Greenwood. On top of that, it was wearing the inside-centre jersey, No 12. I am not joking, this is gospel.

And the coincidences didn't stop there. The lads took great glee in informing me that, according to the race card, Greenwood had shown no real form since 2003 and his niggling injuries made him an ongoing concern. The turf experts' verdict on this fine animal? It won't figure in the shake-up. Imagine my mirth when my four-legged doppelgänger romped in at 7-1.

While Royal Windsor races may not be one of those sporting events you have to visit at least once in your lifetime – such as the Augusta Masters or a Caribbean Test match – where I am going tonight most certainly is. The Tetley's Super League Grand Final at Old Trafford, Leeds against Bradford.

It must be the Northern monkey in me, Blackburn born and bred, but I blooming well love rugby league.

Liberated from the South for a weekend, I can't wait to don my flat cap, leave the whippet at Mum and Dad's, and get myself down to Old Trafford with the other 68,000 pigeon fanciers. Pie and peas at half-time, marvellous. The train ride will be spent supping ale and putting the finishing touches to two fantasy sides that have been rattling around my brain. Team one is made up of the English rugby league three-quarters I would have loved to see stride out at Twickenham with a red rose on their shirt. It is not so long ago that both forms of the game tried their best to ignore each other and such hypothesis was pure fantasy. Thankfully, the cold war between league and union is long since over and both codes are benefiting.

I had the pleasure of training with Wigan, very briefly I must add, back in 1993 as I recovered from surgery, and it was an honour to be around professionals such as Denis Betts and a young Andy Farrell. As a lad, I was amazed by their dedication, hunger and size. These guys could all run, tackle and pass with serious aplomb and we union boys were lagging behind. Times have changed and the gap has closed, the lines between the two codes blurred. Coaches and players are bringing the best of league and welding it into the 15-a-side game. People like Phil Larder for England and Shaun Edwards at Wasps, with others such as Scott Gibbs and Allan Bateman, who were worth their weight in gold for the 1997 touring Lions.

Andy Robinson should be applauded for taking his England

squad up to Headingley to train with the Leeds Rhinos earlier this year. The World Cup in 2007 is closer than we think and we need to be picking the brains of the league guys on everything from ruthless attacking to diehard defence and pinpoint offensive kicking.

Picking my fantasy teams was never going to be easy but, for better or worse, here are the league greats I would have loved to see in the England shirt. Sean Long and Garry Schofield are the half-back pairing, tremendous organisers, distributors and game-break-ers. In the centre are Martin Gleeson and Paul Newlove, power, pace, skill and guile. The back three are Martin Offiah, Jason Robinson and Joe Lydon, as mesmeric, electric, and graceful a trio as ever there was. Almost as impressive is the list of players I had to leave out: Andy Gregory from the old school and Keith Senior from the current crop. I could pick only seven and there is no room for emotion as a selector.

That brings me to the second fantasy team – the modern rugby union players who I reckon would enjoy themselves 'up North'.

The scrum-half would have to be Austin Healey, with Charlie Hodgson outside – these boys could get any back line moving while always looking for that half-gap to emerge. And if the game is tight, each has the crucial component of a rugby league half-back: exquisite kicking. Centres would have to be Jamie Noon and Mike Tindall, with perhaps Ayoola Erinle as a super sub, all no-nonsense defenders with great horsepower and an ability to play in the heavy traffic.

The back three would demand the inclusion of Ben Cohen – his power making him a formidable league exponent – alongside Josh Lewsey, whose lines of running have coaches purring. At full-back every rugby league team need their version of Tony Adams and, for me, there can only be one – Matt Perry, aka 'The Rock'.

Now you will probably have different views, but I don't reckon there are any players there whom selectors of either code would turn their noses up at. Rugby league and union are wonderfully alike and beautifully different. With the old suspicions gone, the two have a lot to offer each other. And that, my punter friends, is something you can put your shirt on.

Shrinking borders

I was lucky that my father played in Italy. As a child I got to see a part of the rugby world that was unknown to many people. I loved it and my days in Rome are the happiest of memories. For rugby players today travel is a given and for the really lazy, all they have to do is wait while the world comes to them.

There was a time in the not too distant rugby-playing past when things exotic and foreign were anathema. Before global tours and international tournaments, the most exciting thing on the calendar was probably a trip down the motorway. In these not so foreign lands, accents thickened, glances grew more askance, and the locals cut the crusts off their sandwiches.

Today's modern rugby player is no longer such an innocent abroad. In fact, turn up at a Premiership game and you will be just as likely to see a New Zealander, Australian or South African as you will a face from the UK or Ireland. The game is global and the best teams are a United Nations minus the mandate to avoid confrontation.

It has not been an overnight revolution. The foundations were laid by players such as Wayne Shelford, Joel Stransky, Michael Lynagh, Philippe Sella and Francois Pienaar. Drawn by the strength of the pound, a new challenge and the passion of the crowd, these men brought a cachet that far outweighed the already impressive sum of their collective caps.

They wanted to be part of our game, and that could only raise its profile, wage levels and professionalism. But they came to us in the twilight of their careers, and for all their class, they were still on the way down. England and its top league was a glorious swansong.

The overseas player stepping off the plane nowadays is a very different beast. Often in the prime of his physical and rugby-playing life, this guy has a point to prove and the chosen way of doing it is by putting a rocket up the pants of all the home-grown talent. Look at this weekend's matches in the Guinness Premiership and you will see strangers doing their best to settle in by unsettling the opposition.

At Bath, there is the blossoming relationship between World Cup winner Butch James and England nearly man, Olly Barkley. So well are they playing that with the retirement of Mike Catt, England's coach Brian Ashton may look no further than Barkley to fill the inside-centre slot. Saracens have the All Black lock Chris Jack; Newcastle anchor their pack with his Kiwi team-mate Carl Hayman. At Worcester, there is Sam Tuitupou, with Chris Latham due to arrive next season.

The list goes on of those who have abandoned the Super 14 and Tri Nations while still in their prime. But for me, the most interesting arrivals, and a pair who ended up going head to head last weekend, are Luke McAlister at Sale and Aaron Mauger at Leicester.

Their confrontation was a key factor in the way the match turned out and highlighted many of the pluses and minuses that follow the overseas players on their foreign adventure.

First up is the fact that some settle in much quicker than others. A couple of weeks is all it takes for some to be wearing the proverbial slippers and raiding their host's drinks cabinet. Others need longer to relax and find their feet.

There is no doubt that McAlister is already very comfortable with Sale. Playing inside him is Charlie Hodgson, one of the game's best distributors, who has been putting the big Kiwi into the space he has been asking for. Muscular and not afraid to go straight up the middle, McAlister has the undentable confidence of a 24-year-old. It does not matter how many weeks he has not played, nor that he knocked on the first ball that he touched. He still called for and kicked the tricky penalty that put Sale in front.

During the first 15 minutes McAlister did not touch the ball, but his contribution was immense. He chased, tackled and organised with such calm determination that the team around him was galvanised. On the day he outplayed Mauger, who is taking longer to settle at Leicester. This does not surprise me as he is a different type of player. A proper outside five-eighth or second fly-half, he kicks off both feet, and needs to understand the players around him before he can relax and make such a telling impact. But I have no doubt he will because that is what the clubs are paying for and Mauger is nothing if not a professional.

This is where the foreign players' real strength lies. The big gestures and the sparkling tries are the sweeteners, the big-game bonus that comes from top quality. What matters are the small, almost unseen things, the fine-tuning and the sense of purpose they bring. Clubs are buying in an ethos and an aura when they put down the big bucks. It is money well spent. The foreign players will observe and comment on what needs to be done.

The changes are subtle and telling. When Saracens scored against Harlequins it was from a glorious backs move that started with Jack leaping high into the air and delivering line-out ball on a plate to his scrum-half. Young players, and those who are keen to learn, will benefit from playing alongside men of this calibre. Their opponents will learn difficult lessons that will also make them better at what they do.

In the past, 'journeyman' was a term that defined a pro who had been around for a while and not quite made it.

Today, it defines the globe-trotting internationals who are pushing teams and skills to unthought-of standards. This is the new planet rugby, and its borders are shrinking all the time.

The foreign legion

If you bring a lot of foreign players into the UK set-up then there will be some odd consequences, not least which country they play for and which nation they refer to as home. In 2007, a set of big-name players were about to qualify for England, sparking a debate which five years later and countless country-hopping internationals later, may seem parochial in its intensity.

Here is a question for you to ponder over a cup of tea, a slice of toast, and some bacon and eggs – what defines Englishness? Do you need a sense of fair play? Should you be able to tell the difference between real ale and Dutch lager? And what about refusing to use an umbrella even when it is raining cats and dogs? Do these attitudes matter? Are they at the core of who we are? Can they be learnt?

Wiser men than me have struggled to define the essence of the English and come up short. Today, with certain football coaches calling for a quota system to protect national talent and with politicians wrestling with the impact of immigration, it seems as if someone's place of birth has suddenly become a super-hot topic.

Rugby is no different, and in the next few months some very good foreign players could have the opportunity to pledge their allegiance to the English cause. Lesley Vainikolo, Riki Flutey and Glen Jackson will all qualify for the national team after having been residents in England for three years. They have not played international rugby union for any other country, and as a result are available for selection.

Vainikolo, the 'Volcano', is Tongan. He is a giant of a man, whose try-scoring prowess is not in doubt. His power off the wing borders on the unnatural. Bradford Bulls fans will tell you that he is one of the best they have had play for them. He is still learning the union ropes, and it is still too early in his switch from rugby league to say he is the finished article, but he is learning and adjusting quickly.

Paul Sackey, Mark Cueto and Josh Lewsey might be ahead of him at the moment, but what if Vainikolo was to produce the kind of form in union that made him a league great? Would it be so wrong if England coach Brian Ashton and Rugby Football Union's elite rugby director Rob Andrew wanted to have a look at him, and brought him into the England set-up?

The same goes for Flutey, a Maori from New Zealand. He has just lacerated the defences of Munster and Llanelli on consecutive weekends, and has been playing some magical rugby at inside-centre. He can pass, he can kick, he can tackle like a back-row forward and he can run like the wind. Again there are players who would push him, not least Toby Flood and Olly Barkley, but it would be difficult not to pick Flutey if he was available.

So far he has been consistent in his view that an England shirt does not interest him, being about as far as possible from the All Black strip that he obviously cherishes. But would it be so bad to try to tempt him over to the white side if the New Zealanders continue to overlook his obvious talents?

And what about Jackson, last year's players' player in the incredibly tough Premiership? Another New Zealander, he has made a huge impact. At fly-half he stands flat on the gain line with unnerving regularity, he can find gaps that most of us would miss, and he kicks his goals.

We know about the other names – Ryan Lamb, Danny Cipriani, Charlie Hodgson and Jonny Wilkinson – but this guy has experience and would be in the mix if he was available to England.

Nationality at the highest sporting levels has always been an interesting, if at times fraught, issue. Sportspeople such as Zola Budd, Kevin Pietersen, Mike Catt, Allan Lamb, Greg Rusedski, Henry Paul, Shane Howarth, Kevin Maggs and Tony Cascarino have all taken big decisions when it comes to their national ties.

I, for one, can understand their motivation. Sportspeople want to play at the highest level, and in today's professional arenas they also need to make the most money they can in the shortest space of time. An England jersey today helps you secure a safer financial future tomorrow.

At the same time, supporters want their team to be the best in the world, with the goal of winning often taking precedence over where the players or coaches were born. Despite a slightly patchy record, England's rugby elite have always taken the moral high ground when comparing themselves to rivals.

In particular, they have accused New Zealand of plundering the South Seas, scouring its paradise isles for talent and packing the All Blacks with Fijians, Samoans and Tongans.

While New Zealand have not broken any rugby laws, the English have always complained that it was not in the spirit of the game, that it was unfair. They have also muttered about the plastic Paddies and kilted Kiwis employed by our Celtic rivals.

So it will be interesting to see how the RFU tackle this spiky issue over the next year or so, because with so many foreign players coming to Europe, and England in particular, it is unlikely to go away any time soon.

For my part, I have always seen myself as one of the lucky ones in that by being born a Lancastrian and the son of a former England player and coach, there was only ever one jersey I could go after. My options were limited and times were different – the world not as small, sport not as global.

In my first representative game for the senior Lancashire side, John Burgess, the great coach and selector, left us in no doubt about where our loyalties should lie: 'Lancashire, the North, England, in that bloody order!'

If only it were still that simple.

For club and country

As soon as a player becomes an asset with a monetary value, the relationship with their club and country changes. Demands are increased and everyone wants their money's worth. It is not unreasonable, but a failure to sort out the problem in the early days of professionalism meant that by 2007, the club and country row was boiling over.

There has been disharmony at the heart of English rugby for too many years. Clubs and the Rugby Football Union have been screeching at each other over who has the stronger hold on players and the noise has been like fingernails dragging down a blackboard.

However, events over the past few days suggest that we may be moving towards peace and quiet. It would seem that the clubs and RFU are now singing from the same hymn sheet and the tune of the day is 'The player comes first'. If that is the case then it is real progress because the two sides have not always seen things in such simple terms.

The RFU's stance has always been that the player must be available to train with the national squad and represent his country, in the best possible physical condition, so that the England team can win. The clubs' view has been that the player must be available for his club whenever and wherever a fixture list takes them, so that his team can be as successful as possible. Both arguments are valid; it is just that the people making them often behaved like jilted lovers who could remember only the bad times and were never going to kiss and make up.

However, the clubs' decision to rest and bench many of the England players picked by Brian Ashton on Tuesday highlights the progress that has been made. The decisions have been taken on an individual basis, on what is right for the player. And that is the right decision for club and country.

The RFU asked for the players to have a break, and it was nice to see them requesting rather than demanding this concession. Talk to people in the know, and they will tell you that the RFU have not always won friends by putting a gun to the head of the clubs.

In the end the only people in the firing line were the players. Now they might have a chance of dodging bullets with their names on. Jonny Wilkinson should be nowhere near a rugby pitch, having just put himself through a rugby wringer for two weeks with virtually no game time under his belt.

Newcastle, who are by no means clear of relegation, have been magnificent in this regard. Everyone can see the value Wilkinson brings to a side and his injuries mean he has hardly played for his club for three years. Yet Newcastle decided it was in no one's interests, especially the bruised Wilkinson's, to send him out again at the earliest opportunity.

Leicester, always looking to the best interests of an individual's rugby and physical development, have also taken the long view with their selection for the game at Worcester this afternoon. Martin Corry would play every day if asked, but he needs looking after in his autumnal years. However, it is not the same for every member of the England squad. Guys like Toby Flood and Mathew Tait need games. They are young and relatively inexperienced, so the opportunity to play for Newcastle against Bristol should be relished. But for the majority of men who pull on the rose shirt, getting a breather is as vital as putting in the hours in the gym and on the training field.

If you want an example of the damage that can be done by pushing players too far, then look at the week after the last World Cup final. Players who had exhausted themselves, physically and mentally, over a six-month period were back on club duty in the UK.

If you wonder why the England team who won the World Cup disintegrated so quickly, do not look to an open-top bus tour or Christmas cocktails at 10 Downing Street. Simply consider what the players had to endure on a rugby pitch in the months after their victory. And while it was the clubs who wanted to throw players straight back into the cauldron of competition, the RFU do not escape blame. Their decision to send an England team to New Zealand and Australia in the summer of 2004 must go down as one of the most myopic a sporting body has ever taken.

The players have also been far from faultless, even if I am a little more understanding of their predicament. A rugby player, by his nature, has chosen to be a professional sportsman because he wants to play and he wants to win, for his club and for his country. If asked to play, then it goes without saying that he will pack his kit bag and get on the team bus. The question is at what time, and at what level of match fitness, should you say no to your club coach without fear of recrimination from selectors and team-mates. Austin Healey coined a nickname for any player who looked like he might be dodging a club game to make sure he was fit for his country. 'SYFE' – Healey pronounced it as if it rhymed with jiffy – stood for Save Yourself For England. What it meant was players not taking the field in an unfit state, when more often than not their under-par performance would add nothing to the team.

If we are really moving towards a time when players can manage their fitness and playing freshness in an open and honest way, then that is a massive leap forward. The clubs should be applauded for their handling of the situation. It is now up to the RFU and players to push ahead with this bright new era.

The softening of positions has not happened overnight. Players and, I suspect, supporters were in an almost catatonic state brought on by the political manoeuvring and posturing taking place on an almost weekly basis. England's desire to get back to the top table of international rugby is evident but it is by no means a foregone conclusion. The events of the past week signal that there is a desire by all parties to make sure the player is looked after. The benefits of that attitude are plain for all to see and are sweet music to my ears.

Selection system off target

It looked as if the club versus country debate had been sorted out. But by 2008, cracks were beginning to appear in the deal that had been brokered. The worry was that small problems could lead to another outbreak of hostilities.

Jonny Wilkinson's injury has highlighted a problem that could cause England a number of serious headaches. He will not be fit to play in November, although it is worth clarifying that Jonny did not dislocate his knee, he dislocated his knee cap. There is a huge difference. Had he dislocated his knee I do not think he would have played again because a man with a medical history like his would have struggled to return, both physically and mentally.

Suffice to say that Wilkinson will not be taking on the rest of the world in November. It is a shame, because with Toby Flood having gone to Leicester, Jonny's game had improved and he was finding some of his old form.

There was less moving about the back line, he had a more pivotal role playing from the first receiver position where he has been kicking superbly from hand, and slotting dropped goals. His place kicking has been sensational and his tackling has been more comfortable as he can defend in the No 10 channel rather than heading out wide.

However, his absence was a pretty easy decision for selectors to make. What is less simple is what their choices are when faced with players who lose their form rather than their ability to stand up unaided. The devil in this case really is in the detail.

In July, Martin Johnson named a senior England squad of 32 players. Based on the terms of the new agreement between the Rugby Football Union and the clubs, the team for England's autumn internationals could only be selected from this group of players. That's a long way out to predict form.

On the one hand, Johnson and his team of coaches must be overjoyed at the amount of time they have to spend with the squad. A gathering in August, five weeks in November, a whole block of sessions together for the Six Nations. They have so much time they will almost be like a club side. Consistency of selection and stability would be guaranteed – a crucial building block in the process of getting a team believing in each other, working for one another.

On the other hand, naming a squad in July hamstrings a selector when they are sitting down four months later. If the England selectors follow the letter of their agreement with the clubs, then they could go into games without their first-choice XV. The problem

Will Greenwood

they have is that Martin can only replace players who are injured or who have disciplinary issues.

Prior to the Wilkinson injury, England were already in the process of bending the rules so that they could get Danny Cipriani back in the side. But the question still remains: what would they do if the form of a player dipped so badly that he was no longer first choice?

This may not have been a question that mattered too much had England not suddenly found themselves dealing with a few under-performing players, most notably at full-back. In the squad, Josh Lewsey and Mathew Tait have been picked to fill the slot. Josh's form has been indifferent. Shaun Edwards blamed him for 12 of the points that Wasps conceded in their Northampton defeat. He also cost them at least seven in the London Irish defeat.

Tait, meanwhile, has moved to Sale so that he could play in one position, and that is full-back. In the opening games he has been wearing the No 15 shirt but has rarely been seen there. Defensively, he plays at outside-centre because the team have been hiding Charlie Hodgson from defensive duties, so we can't see Tait catch up-and-unders or counter-attack because he is never where he should be. Last weekend he started on the wing but defended in the centre. Confused? I bet Tait is. But Sale are second in the league and the club have first option on where you play.

While the chosen two have been scraping around, others have been doing better. Olly Morgan, not ranked in England's top 64 players at the moment, has shown himself to be an almost carbon copy of Matt Perry. Steady under the high ball, he is solid defensively. At Bath, Nick Abendanon is streets ahead of any full-back in terms of attack. He is sharp, elusive, and with an eye for a gap.

The crazy thing is that Morgan and Abendanon are, at this stage, unavailable for November internationals. There is no doubt that

174

the agreement between England and the clubs is hugely positive. It gives the coaches more time with the players, and should lead to more consistency and stability in selection. But it also looks like it could shut doors on players who warrant selection.

Johnson is not the sort of person to moan about having one hand tied behind his back. He will have to work the fringes and the extremities of the rule process just as he did when he was a player. The rest of us will just have to keep our fingers crossed that we don't end up in a situation where injuries are the only way that England can get their best players on the pitch.

The Rules

The rules of rugby, or more precisely the laws of the game, are together a historical document tracing the development of the sport. Initially they were designed to give players, and to a certain extent the supporters, a structure to work within that would give them the maximum enjoyment from the game. That was fine while the players and punters pretty much did what they did for free. But as soon as rugby started heading towards professionalism then the focus of the laws also started to change. Instead of providing an 80-minute wrestling match that appealed solely to the purists, there was a need for spectacle and excitement that would justify the higher ticket prices and sponsorship deals. At the same time, with players getting bigger, stronger and fitter more care has been needed with regards to their safety. Complicating matters has been the seemingly differing views in the northern and southern hemispheres of how the game should be played. The north by all accounts like stodgy forward driven punch-ups that waddle from one side of the field to the other, while the quicksilver southerners prefer to run on their hard, fast pitches, relishing open spaces and scoring tries at a rate of ten a match. What this has meant is that over the past decade the laws of rugby have changed on an annual basis. Some tweaks have been needed and most have been well thought out, others less so. But despite the head scratching that has often accompanied many changes, rugby's rule book is almost certain to continue changing in years to come as the game continues to evolve.

A precious commodity devalued

Following the 2007 World Cup, rugby's ruling bodies were looking at ways of opening up the game. Their argument that more tries were needed has always been something of a bugbear for me.

It is difficult to know who to blame for rugby's obsession with tweaking the laws of the game. Do you single out a player such as David Campese, a genius and showman who has done little since retiring other than lament how dull the English game has become? Do you point the finger at the rugby unions, who fear that fans will turn to other more punter- and point-friendly sports when given the choice between basketball and a wet Friday night in Worcester? Or is it down to us, the supporters who feast on glitzy showbiz programmes and are supposed to have the attention span of a three-year-old filled up on chocolate cake and fizzy pop?

In the end it does not really matter, because regardless of the source, the constant changing serves only to irritate me. Like Nero when Rome was burning, today's rugby emperors seem intent on fiddling. The World Cup – a brilliant six-week tournament that showed how great our game can be – has only just finished and yet here we are again looking to turn a great sport into an all-singing, all-dancing, firework festival of tries, tries and more tries.

I appreciate that I come from the anorak end of the game. I love the subtle intricacies of rugby, the sleight of hand, the sledgehammer aggression, the physical, sinuous grace of top sportsmen moving at speed. What makes me even more frustrated is that the opening weekend of the Heineken Cup served only to reinforce how strong European rugby has become and how much it has to offer. Look at the English game, and the emergence of top-quality fly-halves.

There are some wonderful players out there. Gloucester's Ryan Lamb had a great game last week, still a fraction short on physicality but already much more of a force than last year. In much the same way you have to admire his dedication to building muscle, so you should admire how the skills are developing. His distribution, his line breaks, his kicking out of hand for territory, his threaded kick for big Lesley Vainikolo's try put him right in the mix for an England place.

At Wasps there is Danny Cipriani. He has attitude and talent in abundance. Knock him down and he gets straight back up again. To be able to fill Alex King's shoes so well, and to lead a team who come from 10 points down twice against Munster shows you as much about his character as you need to know. Danny has details to improve on. He too often passes without fixing the defenders, allowing them to drift off him and on to the outside backs too quickly, but I am being picky. It's his fault for setting the bar so high.

What is remarkable about the youngsters is that they are starting to hog the column inches and it takes time to get down to the likes of Charlie Hodgson in the European Challenge Cup (and we won't even get round to talking about Jonny Wilkinson, Toby Flood and Shane Geraghty). If the new boys want a lesson in pinpoint accuracy and distribution off either hand, then Hodgson is still the master. But what they bring is a freshness of approach.

The thing I enjoy about them and the teams they are playing in is their vision, talent and flair. They are adapting to defensive systems on the hoof, trying to find a way through, round, over or under. Unfettered and full of youthful enthusiasm, they are beginning to work out new ways and systems to score tries. It is great to see sides improvise and adapt to what's in front of them.

What is even more exciting is that players across Europe are drawing on their talents and trying increasingly smart moves to get across the tryline. Ronan O'Gara's deft kick with the outside of his foot for Shaun Payne's try against Wasps was as good a piece of play as you'll see, as was his pass that put Lifeimi Mafi through a hole for Rua Tipoki's opener. And remember that this was against a Wasps defence that has been so impressive.

For Leinster, it was Felipe Contepomi who breathed life into the team. His confidence, swagger and comfort on the ball was such that Brian O'Driscoll and Gordon D'Arcy were immediately back in threatening mode. They all combined for a try from a set piece, which is apparently impossible to do in the modern game. Even in this land of the giants, accuracy of pass, legitimacy of decoy, angles of run and timing of delivery can work wonders. Ever bigger and stronger players may be the future, but they can also be a weakness. Alesana Tuilagi on this occasion was caught narrow, wanting to put a South Sea Island hit in, and before he could blink his opposite man was diving in for a try. Elsewhere in the competition it was Regan King doing it for Llanelli, and this weekend it will be fascinating to watch him try to open up Wasps' defences.

For all my puff and blunder, I'm no innocent abroad. I know that rugby is not a perfect game, that matches can on occasion be a little slow. But doesn't it make the great games all that more thrilling when they come around like they did last week? We should enjoy it when defences smother a team and make it difficult for the opposition to move. That is as much a skill as scoring a try. We should also learn to take pleasure from watching teams and players evolve and improve. That's as much fun as the 10-try romps.

Rugby's great and good should not create space for the sake of it. They should enjoy clever young players and coaches working out how to slip off the shackles and poke one eye out from under the blindfold. Europe's best teams will work out how to find space in a tight, packed environment if you give them time. Brilliance is a rarity that is hard earned. That's why it's so special and unforgettable when it happens. Make it easier, turn it into an everyday occurrence, and we will end up devaluing rugby's most precious commodity.

The blame game

For the 2008-09 season the laws saw some significant changes. And while many teams were adapting quickly, others were struggling and hiding their continuing problems behind a smokescreen of complaints about the new rules.

The players who do well are the ones who manage to adapt when faced with a new set of parameters and requirements.

Today, if anything, it is more important than in the past as teams are having to digest new rules on an almost annual basis. My view is pretty simple – old laws, new laws, who cares? Use your head, make the right decisions, and you will win. Miss your cue, lose concentration, and you will lose. Moaning about the rule changes is not going to alter anything, and they are here to stay for a season at least.

My personal verdict on the new laws is mixed. Some, such as allowing the collapsing of a maul, I hate. For a forward, sitting at the back of a moving maul – they lovingly called it the chariot – knowing when to break off and wreak havoc was an art. As a player, it used to terrify me when my pack were on the receiving end.

Another change I dislike is the decision to let teams put as many players in a line-out as they want. This makes it much harder to get an advantage from a penalty that has been kicked into touch because the opposition can just stack the subsequent line-out.

Shortened line-outs, which were designed to get the ball moving and back-row forwards powering up the middle of the park, may become a thing of the past because the other team will not let you win the ball in the first place. What was once a great opportunity for a good platform is now a bun fight.

However, there are positives. I like the fact that teams can now take a quick line-out without the throw-in having to be perpendicularly perfect.

I am happy that players will no longer be able to pass back into the 22 and then kick straight to touch. I am looking forward to sides using the extra five metres they have from attacking scrums now that defences have to stand further back.

There is both good and bad in the changes, a curate's egg of tweaking that makes it hard to get too angry about them. Except that is, when they lead to a bigger problem and something that really gets my goat. The simple truth is that too many people are blaming the new rules for their poor decision-making during a game. I want to reiterate my previous point – you use your head and you win, make crass judgment calls and you lose. Two tries were scored last weekend which had everyone jumping on the 'new laws are rubbish' bandwagon. Sadly, they had less to do with the changes and more to do with moronic decision-making. Harlequins scored within a minute against Saracens as Dave Strettle crossed from a midfield scrum in the Sarries 22.

Danny Care darted and delivered, Strettle stepped and scored. Was it really so easy just because the defence were five metres further away? I doubt it.

One of the first lessons you are told as a team is that when you are defending a blind side close to your own line it is almost impossible for a blind-side flanker to catch a fizzing scrum-half in a race for the corner. Saracens had Chris Jack on the blind-side flank, a second row turned flanker. Outside of him it was a simple two versus two match-up.

Saracens were in trouble from the moment they decided not to stack their blind-side defence. A team have to overload the short side when defending their line. I don't buy the excuse that the open side is then short of bodies, because the scrum-half stays there to cover the first man round.

Simplistic, maybe. Effective, absolutely, and until teams learn to follow this old-fashioned advice we will keep hearing rubbish about how the new laws make it too easy for sides to score from scrums.

At the line-out, things were little better. In another game, London Irish crashed over from a line-out that started five metres from the Wasps line. The new-rule bandwagon rolled again, but look closely and you will see that a poor call was at fault.

Wasps put five men in the line-out – Irish put in six, as they are now allowed to do. Nick Kennedy was stationed at the front for London Irish, and he is one of the European line-out masters. He saw Wasps stand three men at the front and two at the back and figured he had a free gamble. He must have felt sure Wasps had cut the line-out so that they could throw beyond the 15-metre line to their awaiting back-row forwards.

Imagine his surprise when, as he jumped just for something to do, Wasps threw the ball short and he was able to put enough pressure on Wasps so that they could only tap back 50-50 ball. It hit the deck and was won by an Irish player at the back, Chris Hala'ufia, where he and his team-mates outnumbered Wasps.

Seven points for nothing, maybe, but down to human error, not bad laws. Rugby is a sport for brawn that can't function without brain. Teams and players need to switch their grey matter on and stop blaming other people for their shortcomings.

Bloodgate

This was one of the most shocking incidents to ever happen in English club rugby. In n2009, Harlequins, my old club, were found to have cheated, to have lied about an injury to their player with the aim of getting a goal kicker back on the field so he could kick the winning points. What happened that day changed the view that many people had of our sport and caused many others to question if they wanted to be part of how it was developing.

I want the rugby season to start, I want rugby on the back pages for all the right reasons.

The sport is at its lowest ebb right now, on its knees. It's being laughed at and scorned. But this is not a time to grovel for forgiveness, to be weak, it is time for us to face up to the problems and put our house in order.

Where to start? The 'Bloodgate' affair has cast a long shadow over the start of the new season, but it's right that it should have done.

I was working for Sky on that fateful March afternoon when Harlequins took on Leinster and from the moment I saw the images of Tom Williams coming off for Nick Evans I felt my old club would be lucky to be in the Heineken Cup this season.

The use of a joke shop blood capsule, the manner in which it was done and the extent of the cover-up has shocked everyone in the game. And no matter who they were trying to protect, it was wrong. They should have put their hands up from the start and if they were to go on and win the Heineken Cup, as things stand right now, I would find it hard to celebrate.

No question, there will be disappointment among the players at losing a manager like Dean Richards. He took them to second in the league and while I can't defend what he did, he is a hard man and a brilliant coach who got more out of players than they felt they had inside them.

As for Tom, I am certain the players will come around to him once he returns. They know they might have found themselves in the same situation and sport moves on quickly.

There is still a lot of work to do to repair the sport's image on this front. But the initial reactions from the authorities are encouraging. The introduction of the voluntary code which will allow opposition doctors to check players coming off with blood injuries should prevent future fake blood incidents.

I am delighted the issue of uncontested scrums has been dealt with. A full complement of men who perform the hardest job in rugby is the minimum requirement to safeguard this most Trojan of jobs. If you run out of front-row forwards, which is what would have happened to the Lions in the second Test, then that is unfortunate and you must continue with 14 players. This has been trialled in France and the number of uncontested scrums has virtually disappeared.

But it's not just been about fake injuries. Gouging must be abolished and one-year bans must be the minimum for anyone transgressing.

On the issue of substitutes, there is little to choose between rugby league and rugby union – the power is such in both sports that we cannot compare to yesteryear – and rolling subs would not detract from the spectacle. Let us borrow from our friends and put in place a system that works. This is a must, because the game is becoming increasingly physical. The Lions series took it all to a new level that the Tri-Nations continued.

Scrums are killing the game

In the wet, dark months of midwinter, it looked as if English rugby was coming to a standstill, matches broken up by poor scrums. The problem was getting so bad that by January 2011 there was a lot of talk that more rules were needed and that something drastic had to be done.

Imagine two tons of meat, muscle and bone colliding. You can almost hear the thump it would create. The sudden rush of breath, past gritted teeth, from the mouths of the players involved. The groans, the grunts, the sheer bloody-mindedness it would take to do it time and again and still enjoy it. That, my friends, is the scrum that dominates our game of rugby union.

A mass of muscles, body fat, and lumpily painful bits, it is where a dislike for our fellow man ferments. In its dark recesses an inch counts and a yard becomes a hard-fought victory that is savoured by those who understand how much they have risked to make it happen. I don't profess to understand it. I am scared by it, but it is the core around which the game is built.

When rugby league went professional, they messed about with the scrum and their bastardised version still damages their reputation and brings smirks of derision from union purists.

For my part, I love the scrum, so it pains me to say this but, in its current form, it is killing the game. The scrum is in danger of becoming a black hole into which match time disappears, and supporters will end up wishing they had stayed at home to watch the *Murder She Wrote* marathon.

Some 20 per cent of all matches are taken up by the endless resets, collapses, standing up, falling over and general messing about. If a bookie offered me odds on the first scrum being penalised and never actually taking place in all of the Premiership matches, then that is a bet I would take on every week. In five of the six games last weekend the first scrum was penalised.

It has become risible and the problem is as simple as the techniques involved are complicated. Scrums are collapsing because people are cheating.

Talk to any coach in the country, and they are always looking to get an edge at the scrum. They either want to get the nudge on early, or move the right side up, or the left side up. They may have lost a player to the sin-bin, and want to waste time.

When I was playing in the league, my team had a plan in place for when we lost players to the sin-bin. The first scrum they pushed early, the result a reset. The second they went to ground, reset. The third they scrummaged properly. The idea was that we could waste about two minutes of sin-bin time doing this.

All very valuable in the game context, all very smart, and all very much done by the majority of the professional sides, and a lot of the ones lower down the leagues as well.

Before the match between Cardiff and Northampton, Blues coach Dai Young complained about the Saints' skulduggery and their boring in on the hooker.

Talk to any of the front-row forwards I have, and they say they would be surprised if a team didn't try to bore in and force the hooker up and out of the scrum. At worst allowing you to dominate the scrum, at best, you can win a penalty because it looks like the opposition are standing up early.

In the world of the scrum, it's a double win because not only do you get the points, but you also get one over on the opposition and referee. Which sadly, seems to be happening more often than not nowadays.

One of the biggest issues is the arbitrary refereeing of the scrum area. After watching a weekend of matches, for every 10 penalties or free kicks awarded for infringements at the scrum, I estimate that six or seven could have just as easily gone the other way.

I asked an expert. It's a lottery and it's one that is worth having a punt at because it can lead to points or a sending to the sin-bin.

I don't want to put more pressure on the referees than necessary, but are we (and I use the term collectively as I believe we all have a role to play in this game we love) doing enough to educate them on the intricacies of the front row and the dark arts of the scrum? Are we using the retired masters of their universe, players such as Sean Fitzpatrick, Jason Leonard and Brian Moore, to shed light on what is going on?

Don't get confused by the fact that there are plenty of former front-row forward coaches out there. Their job is to keep the myth going that it is impossible to understand because it allows them to steal the inches they need. Like career criminals they understand that they may need to do some time in chokey. But they also appreciate that the rewards are enough to make it worth their while.

The Rugby Football Union should turn to the retired experts for their views on what needs to be done. I would love to see a scrum task force put together.

Give them a cool name and send them off round the country like a pack of modern-day Edward Woodwards and let them equalise the scrum problem. They wouldn't be the prettiest bunch, more beer-barrel chested than six-packed but, by God, they would get the job done.

Referees would no longer need to award free kicks on a rotation basis and forwards would know their number was up. Because something needs to be done.

When the scrum works properly it is the foundation to the game. It underpins the culture in France and Argentina. It warms the cockles of an Englishman's heart when it lets us bully the fleet-footed Aussies.

And it gives the game a physical focal point that lets both sets of forwards fight it out in one of the purest forms of gladiatorial confrontation that still exists in today's sanitised sporting world. Simply put, we can't do without it.

So please, in 2011, help me eradicate the blight of collapsing scrums. Send me your ideas, petition the RFU, let's all do something fast.

Otherwise, with draconian options, we could end up with what those cowardly three-quarters have been calling for all along – a game where scrums have no purpose and where the fine art of pushing has died a sad and untimely death.

Rugby rewritten

Getting the laws of rugby right takes time, but by September 2010 it looked as if a revolution was taking place. Lawmakers had made a fundamental change to how referees view the breakdown and the impact was spectacular.

This season could be the most important in the history of rugby union. We are entering a 12-month period that will define the game's future, change the view we had of it looking back, and put down the foundations for global domination that will see rugby challenge the biggest spectator sports.

The reason for my bullish optimism is the quality of rugby played in the recent Tri-Nations tournament. It was breathless stuff – literally. I have never seen rugby played at such pace for such a sustained period of time.

Players were moving the ball from all parts of the field, preferring to run rather than kick, daring the defence to stop them if they could. Props were flinging passes that three-quarters would have been proud of, backs were rucking and taking contact.

This was rugby turned on its head. I was getting text messages from friends, both rugby fans and sometime viewers, who could not believe what they were seeing. They all talked about the spectacle of what was going on. This was a style of rugby that could draw people away from football, from Twenty20 cricket, from anything that sold itself as fast, sexy and exciting. Rugby was suddenly seat-of-your-pants stuff that you didn't have to be a purist to understand.

The main driver of this shift has been the new rules and interpretations at the breakdown that were introduced at the turn of 2010. It took a while for teams and coaches to come to terms with them but they now have and it has caused a revolution. Simply put, it has given the team with the ball a greater chance of keeping it in contact.

Over the past few years, the defence has been in the ascendancy. Players like Richie McCaw, George Smith and Heinrich Brussow have been the match-winners. They waited like muggers to tackle the player with the ball.

They hit low with their shoulders, swung themselves round and back on to their feet, got their hands on the ball, and either won a turnover or a penalty when the attacker was judged to have held on for too long. It was legalised robbery, and it was killing the game. So the rules were changed, again, to a chorus of boos and accusations of tinkering for the sake of it. I forgive the naysayers because no one, myself included, could have imagined just how far-reaching the changes would be. Today, the tackler must roll away, and the player with the ball has longer to play it back. In effect, the rules have neutralised the limpets at the breakdown, and given teams with the guts and lungs to attack a better chance of success.

As a result, a player has to pass, ruck, maul and move. Bulked-up players are having to strip down every ounce of fat because the game is moving so fast everyone has to keep up. Teams are revising the way they play.

Take the kick-off. For years, the fly-half would look to stick it up high, giving the chasers time to get to it. Today, they are hitting it hard and low for two reasons: first, their chasers are quicker than ever before; second, it takes the opposition's catchers and lifters out of the game. Instead of the static aerial ballet, we now have a start that is more like the murder ball I used to play at school. You cannot allow the opposition any kind of ball, they won't kick it back to you. It whizzes in, gets picked up and the hits start coming.

It is fearsome stuff, not least because the way of tackling has also shifted. If you want to turn someone over today, then the best way to do it is to hit them front on. You either want to dislodge the ball, or hit someone so hard you knock them backwards. Let them get past your shoulder, get in behind you, and the new rules will mean you are chasing backwards, scrabbling to stop an attack that can keep going until there is either a mistake or a score of one type or another. Want to know how far this can go? Then how about this – scrums and most definitely line-outs could become side issues of lessening importance. It's not that the scrums will be depowered, the line-outs ignored, it's just that if you don't make a mistake, or kick the ball out, then why have them? The new rules mean you have a very good chance of retaining the ball and scoring.

The game in England is going to have to adapt quickly. Will it mean a shift away from the power and defensively strong sides such as Leicester? Will it mean the death of the drift defence and a reliance on the blitz and nothing else? It's too early to tell, but what is certain is that sides willing to have a go, to run, to chance their arm and bust their lungs, will have much more of an opportunity than before to give a team like the Tigers a black eye.

There will be surprises in this club season and it will be thanks to the latest rules. Luckily, England's management and players will have a chance to see how far they have come and still have to go in the upcoming autumn internationals.

Not least in terms of their fitness. They can get to half-time and seem out on their feet. However, that is going to change, not least because there is a World Cup coming up.

The next year will see some of the hardest fitness training ever, and players will change shape and develop new skills. And while that sounds good, it is not all great news. What I worry about is that the diversity in shape and size that made rugby so special will have to be sacrificed to produce players that can compete on an international level. The lumpy, slow, scrimmaging prop may well disappear, as will the hunt for the seven-foot second row, or light but lightning-fast three-quarter. In their place will come the robo-player who can do all the physical stuff, sidestep like a winger, and run a sub-10-second 100 metres. The dark arts, the real technical stuff that purists so love, will disappear because the ball will never be in one place long enough for any niggle or cunning to develop. And the gap between the elite and the rest of the rugby-playing public will grow even wider.

When I was playing, every club player, no matter where they played, had the crazy notion that they could get a call-up to the national squad. All it would take was a few injuries, and you could be plucked from obscurity in the Twickenham crowd and thrust into the England side. And you know what? They could probably have done it, they could have survived for a while at least without being found out. OK, they wouldn't make headlines, but they had a chance of doing the job. Back then, the top players really were like the rest of us. There was always that glimmer of hope and ambition.

Today, Twickenham Man wouldn't make it to the first break in play. The first hit would put you in hospital and you'd be glad to get there with only a few broken bones. At least you would get to watch the rest of the game on TV, which is where this new style of rugby is most at home. It is the spectacle that the game has longed for and said it needs to really become a world-beater. With the World Cup coming up, the scene is set for a wonderful 12 months. Just don't expect rugby to ever be the same again.

An old foe can teach us a lesson

Player safety is the most important thing on a rugby field. But often a law with the best of intentions can have an unforeseen effect. By December 2011 it was becoming clear that a lot of people had very different views on how to police spear tackles and eradicate them from rugby.

The spear tackle is sweeping through the game of rugby. Or rather it would seem that way if you believed all the noise and news on the topic. Suspensions, yellow and red cards, high-profile incidents, it's all been happening over the past few months.

It is not an easy topic to cover as very few things divide opinion quite so much. I still remember feeling stunned in Auckland during that semi-final between Wales and France. I was not sure what was happening, a bit unsighted, only to see young Sam Warburton appear on the screen in the stands, jacket on, the damning strapline at the bottom of the screen informing us that one of the finest players at the World Cup, a nation's leader, had been sent off.

A game-changing, life-changing moment. The tackle that got Warburton dismissed still is not settled. Was there intent, wasn't there, injury or not?

The letter of the law says Alain Rolland was right. I rate and respect Rolland more than any other referee on the planet. It does not mean the law he has followed is right.

Let me qualify my comments. I am not going to argue that players should be put in harm's way, that an already dangerous game should become more fraught. That is a line that must never be crossed, and safety is at the forefront of every player's mind, retired or not. I do not take it lightly; I nearly lost my life on a rugby field.

However, on the subject of the tip tackle there needs to be a shift in how it is viewed. Throughout the whole process of the tip or spear tackle we look at everything through the prism of the tackler's intent.

We are focusing on whether he or she lifts the player beyond the horizontal, how they drive through, what the mechanics of their bodies are during the contact and with it the impact he or she has on the player they are hitting.

So far so clear, not least my view that any player who wilfully lifts another and drives them headlong into the turf should see red and serve a long punishment. But it takes two to tackle, and the actions of the player being tackled are overlooked far too often. We seem to be ignoring them, what they are doing during the tackle process. We only seem to see the point of contact with the ground and then, most likely, through a wince or hand that hides our eyes.

We react with emotions and fear and often this clouds our judgment. It is natural, and human. Pain is not a pleasant thing to watch and the damaging of an opponent is not why supporters or players love rugby. And yet, if we are being fair to both sides, we must think about how the tackled player behaves and reacts at the point of contact.

They are not on a suicide mission, keen to drive their own heads and shoulders into the turf, nor are they play-acting to win a cheap penalty and get an opponent sent off. But very often they are doing something that contributes to a spear tackle occurring.

To understand what they do we need to think about the mentality of the attacking player and the emphasis placed on retaining the ball at the point of contact. When you carry the ball into a head-on tackle and lose the point of contact, you are going to go backwards. Your legs will start to lose contact with the ground, and your balance and movement will be suddenly shunted into reverse and turned bum over tip.

The first thing that goes through a professional player's mind is not a fear of injury, they spend years unlearning this response. Rather, it is getting the ball back to their team-mates in the best possible way they can.

If they fail to do this, they cause problems for their side. Lose that tackle, concede a turnover, a penalty and the game can swing. World Cups have been won and lost on such fine margins. So back to that initial contact, and the player who is going backwards, their legs out of the game, and their mind shouting to them to get the ball safely to their colleagues. The one thing they can do is move their upper body, and the best way to negate the tackler is to get both it and the ball on the ground as fast as possible. Get to deck quickly, stay in the traffic and you can still win the point of contact.

You can be surrounded and helped out, the ball can be protected. Get driven backwards and you lose contact with your support. Team-mates cannot help you because the breakdown has to be entered from the wrong side and the momentum is with the opposition rushing forward. Your team is suddenly in trouble and a professional player is trained not to let that happen.

So they fall back on their training and as soon as their bodies are in a bad position, with no leg power, they try to force their bodies down to the ground. I have no doubt about it, I have watched hit after hit, tape after tape.

A player being tackled can directly influence the outcome of a tackle and make it look like a spear tackle through no fault of their own other than a willingness to protect the ball, their team and themselves.

I sat with Shaun Edwards during the second round of the Heineken Cup and we talked about spear tackles, how they were happening and what could be done to improve the game's handling of the issue. I appreciate that he is also in the Wales camp and don't want this to become a lament for the cruelty of that night in New Zealand. But if I could talk to one man about the intricacies of tackling then the Wales defence coach would have to be that man.

We agreed that the system of 'being put on report' that is used in rugby league would go a long way to sorting out the issue. It is a very clever use of the rules and with it the ability to maintain control of the game.

A referee who sees what he believes to be an act of foul play but is not sure of its severity can highlight the incident immediately to independent reviewers. After the final whistle these adjudicators can then study each case closely to understand intent and any illegality. Let us not fool ourselves that this is a soft measure, because the tackles in rugby league can be much more brutal than union. At the same time, the players are under no illusion that if in post-match reviews they are found guilty of attempting to harm a player, then they will serve a long ban. So the threat is there, the knowledge of punishment is there. Players know there can be no evading justice and modify their behaviour on the field.

And while it will not eradicate the bad tackle, it will at least give players and referees a chance to evaluate a situation coolly and calmly.

And that is surely in the interest of everyone in the game.

The Boss

Being the manager of the England team must be one of the most fulfilling and toughest of any jobs in the world. England's fantastic resources and huge talent pool are off-set by the expectations of the public and a governing body that demands success and is often impatient with those who fail to deliver. I have seen the demands of the job up close when my father held the position back in the Eighties, and I can promise you that even in the amateur era it produced sleepless nights and fraught moments. As a player, I have worked under some of the best. When they get it right, the manager is someone who can define an era and create a team that is worth more than the sum of its parts. When they get it wrong they suddenly understand just how fickle sporting success and adulation can be.

The pursuit of Woodward

Sir Clive Woodward was the man who enabled England to win the 2003 World Cup. His focus on perfection created a set-up that allowed the players to shine. What he did was revolutionary and England have struggled to create something as effective ever since. That's why in March 2006, after a number of difficult years, there were increasing calls to get Woodward back as manager of the national team in the hope that he could work his magic once again.

Discussions between senior members of the Rugby Football Union and Sir Clive Woodward about the former coach taking charge of England's defence of the World Cup next year have been taking place for several months, since long before England finished their disappointing 2006 Six Nations campaign with a hat-trick of defeats.

My sources tell me that should Woodward return, his position would give him total responsibility for English rugby from schools through to the national team.

The negotiations have intensified in recent weeks, and there has even been talk of Woodward taking control of a war chest to ensure that clubs are compensated for losing key players in the lead-up to the World Cup, which takes place in France next September.

Reappointing Woodward, now director of football at Southampton FC, would prove a controversial decision, especially as his performance at the helm of last year's Lions tour to New Zealand was widely criticised.

Never one to compromise or take the easy option, Woodward has as many enemies as admirers. There has been much speculation that he might be appointed in a coaching role, but according to sources close to the talks, this has never been an option.

Woodward, who masterminded England's World Cup victory in Australia in 2003, would never wear a tracksuit again because it would serve no purpose for him or English rugby.

The only way he would come back would be as director of rugby with a place on the RFU board. That may sound a big demand, but there have been rumours of significant restructuring at Twickenham for some time.

Fran Cotton recently revealed that Andy Robinson, the head coach, wanted to remove Chris Spice, England's performance director. This is a position that for some time has been stripped of any real power and must be nearing the end of its life.

The 'overlord' position that Woodward would require is not totally new. Cotton, albeit under the title of chairman of Club England, used to wield the sort of control that the board see Woodward undertaking.

Remember it was Cotton who brought Woodward into the England fold in 1997 and it was Cotton who ultimately decided that he should stay in charge after the ignominious exit from the World Cup in 1999.

The decision at the time was viewed as a backward step, but Cotton had access to all the information; he knew what Woodward brought to the party and knew he would ultimately deliver.

Cotton was a hard-headed businessman with an intimate

knowledge of the game and a full understanding of what was required to succeed. That was why he could call the shots. Since his resignation in May last year there has been no one willing to take on that responsibility or fight the players' corner.

According to my sources, it was made clear to the RFU that Woodward would come back only if he had complete responsibility for the appointment of managers at each and every age group, and would be involved in choosing the coaching staff at every level, from the top down.

It seems that people who have jobs within the England set-up would have to reapply for their positions. The right individuals would be brought in, regardless of obstacles or demands.

My understanding is that the talks between the RFU and Woodward also touched on the subject of a considerable fund, financed by the RFU, that could be used to create a partnership between the top clubs and England. Clubs would be properly remunerated in a fair manner for releasing their players for England duty.

To create a World Cup-winning side England need considerably more time than the coaches are being given. In terms of time to prepare and rest time, England lag behind almost every nation bar France.

Cotton said in 2005: 'If the status quo remains, I think England will do well to get past the quarter-finals at the next World Cup'.

'And the best way to ensure that England have the access to players they need is to pay the clubs who employ them. Putting serious money on the table would be a big call by the RFU – and so would bringing back Woodward.'

Getting rid of the coaches would be a short-term move that Cotton called little more than 'shuffling the deck chairs around the Titanic'.

The mantra of Martin Johnson's World Cup-winning side was often that the difference between winning and losing was doing 100 things one per cent better. Nowadays English rugby seems to be doing 100 things one per cent worse.

It would be true to say that Woodward's reappointment could be just what the national side need. It could also be an unwelcome distraction. A number of Woodward's former players have voiced both disapproval and backing for the notion.

In my experience, as a player who won a World Cup medal under Woodward, the RFU would be hard pressed to find a more worthy candidate to run a world-class sporting institution. It is time the RFU backed up all their talking with action to set England on the road to winning the World Cup once more.

Time to move on

Andy Robinson was the man who took over as England manager after Sir Clive Woodward. A tough job was made harder as results went against him and England's style of play was criticised. By November 2006, and following a defeat to Argentina, the calls for him to be replaced reached a crescendo.

Andy Robinson is not the man he used to be. Watching his post-match interviews was like seeing a ghost. The old Andy was never happier than when he was talking about sport, any sport. He would put on his tracksuit and play warm-up games of touch rugby with the boys, in the thick of things, having a laugh.

True, he's called 'Growler', but that was more about him wanting his packs to be the nasty eight-man war machines that prompted the New Zealand press to label them white orcs on steroids. He wasn't the funniest guy to be around. So what? As players, we liked him and respected him. We never doubted his commitment and appreciated the hard work he put in, the extra hours spent improving the handling and skills of players like Phil Vickery and Trevor Woodman. His dedication brought out the best in the players and he was instrumental in England winning the World Cup. That's why it is upsetting to see Andy today struggling under the weight of the team's poor performances.

On Saturday, after England had again lost, this time to Argentina, he told reporters that he was not going to discuss his position and whether he was going to resign or get the sack. When he was pressed on the issue it looked as if he was going to walk off, before he regained his composure and stood firm. Too little, too late. His mask had slipped and we had been given a glimpse of the turmoil he must be going through.

It must be hard to deal with the criticism that has been hurled his way and I can understand why he might feel like swinging back. But part of the job is talking to the press and after England's dismal run of results people have a right to start asking whether or not he is the right man for the job. Especially when Robinson survived the recent cull that saw his number two, three and four head for the door.

From the crowd's reaction at Twickenham, many people now feel it is time for a change at the top. The key question is whether that feeling has spread to the dressing room. Martin Corry was vocal in his support for his boss, but I find it hard to believe that

Robinson has the complete confidence of the players in the squad. How are people like Charlie Hodgson and Pat Sanderson going to feel at training today after they were pulled off the field following mistakes? What will be going through the minds of the young players who will now be terrified of dropping a ball for fear that their international careers could be over even before they have started?

Robinson is a fighter, but he has not always won his battles as England's supremo. Instead he has allowed the terms to be dictated to him from on high at the Rugby Football Union. I don't think Robinson understands the politics of his job as well as he understands the coaching. His reaction to the press questions about his future clearly showed this.

What England need now is someone who will inspire the players to play out of their skins and punch above their weight. For all his qualities, I just do not feel that Andy Robinson, the new or the old, is that man.

Martin Johnson: England are lucky to have him

When Martin Johnson got the job of England manager, questions were asked about his ability. Having played with him at Leicester and England, I had a clear understanding of why he would be able to deliver.

There are a number of misconceptions about Martin Johnson that stop people from seeing the whole man. True, he has a frightening presence on the pitch, but in a brutal physical sport to truly win the respect of your peers and rivals takes more than a furrowed brow and clenched fist.

To do that you need brains, commitment and a little something special, all three of which Johnno has in spades. If you want to understand the Martin mystique a little better, then watch the first kick-off at the World Cup final in 2003.

Jonny Wilkinson kicks long right and the team hare off after it. There were genuine speedsters chasing after it, quick back rowers, Josh Lewsey out on the edge of the forwards. The Australian Nathan Sharpe catches the ball just inside his 22, his back to England.

He goes to spin and turn and is clattered by Martin Johnson. There is no way he should have been there, but he was leading his team as he always did, from the front, setting the tone.

Pre-match reminders about work rate are accompanied by a look into each player's eyes that is difficult to match for intensity. He does not chatter needlessly.

Martin understands that rugby is a simple game, but that does not come from a lack of intellect. If anything, he is one of the best students of the game I have come across.

His life was spent in the dark recesses of the front five, and yet he understood three-quarter moves better than many a world-class winger. For some backs it took five or six goes to get what we were trying to do. Not Johnno – he just needed to be told once and could do it without rehearsal. He loved to play about, to experiment.

And he would ask questions, he wanted to know why we were considering switching players into different positions for the move. Was it because of different skill sets, abilities, running lines? He is a second row!

He shouldn't know or care what happens out in the backs.

Trouble is, he loves the game and wants to understand it so that his teams can win. The more he knows, the less chance there is of making a mistake, the more opportunity for winning matches.

I chatted to him not long ago about the 2003 final and his memories. Forget the good, he is still cross with himself for failing to get the right message across in his half-time chat. England were the side playing most of the rugby, and Martin told us to do more of the same.

This was a mistake, he has now decided. What he wanted us to focus on was getting the next score, no matter how we did it. Had we done that, had he got his message right, he is convinced that we would have won the game well before extra time was required.

Hear him talk about it today and you hear of his anger and frustration at an error, and this is long after his winner's medal has been tucked away.

Martin had an innate understanding of what was going on around him both on and off the field. While others were losing their heads, he remained calm and in control. During his reign as England captain there were some difficult situations, not least the players' strike.

He never compromised his principles and he was able to deal with, and deflect a lot of the rugby politics that came with the captain's job. He was able to rein in Sir Clive Woodward when needed, and could deal with the RFU top brass.

What was never in doubt was that his team would always come first, that he would do everything in his power both on and off the field to make it a success. Often that meant taking a back seat and allowing others to take the lead.

When he took over the captaincy in 1999, one of the first things he needed to do was develop the role of trusted lieutenants. Lesser men would have worried about their position being undermined.

Martin trusted others to make decisions, he backed them to make his team better.

In his new role for England he will need all of the skills that made him the player he was, not least his cracking sense of humour, and some extra ones for good measure. The spotlight will be harsher than ever before and the barbs will be sharp and unforgiving.

Not every great player can make the change from pitch to meeting room but I would put my money on Martin Johnson making the grade.

He is a team man, his own man, a great man. England are lucky to have him.

A leader among men

Martin Johnson was the best captain I ever played with and I backed him for the job of England manager. I still think he was the right man for the job. But the skills and honesty that made him so good as captain ultimately meant that he could not carry on as manager. A man who was ruthlessly honest about his shortcomings was never going to tolerate the errors that he made.

Like it or not, a rugby field is where a player wins respect. I have played for coaches and managers who never won international caps. I have rated them highly, enjoyed their company and loved their insights. But I wouldn't follow them to the ends of the earth.

Only a very few people can instill that kind of loyalty and for me, outside of family, it only comes when you have stood next to a person and faced down your fears and enemies. Martin Johnson is one of those people. When I first played with Johnno at Leicester he was friendly and distant all at the same time. You had to show your mettle on the pitch, and only then would he open up. I got lucky. In the first season of 1996-97 we made a Heineken Cup final and I was in his midweek team to South Africa for the Lions series and nearly dying on a field helped. Johnno obviously reckoned I could do a job for him and I was in.

It changed my life and I am not embarrassed to say that his backing turned me from a skinny player with a bit of talent into a World Cup winner. You wanted to do your best for Johnno the captain. He gave trust, 'you look after the backs, I'll look after the forwards' and this let you gain in confidence and grow as a person. Surrounded by his team, his players, you could see the skills that Johnno had. No matter what has been written about his strategies, he is one of the sharpest British rugby minds I have met. Put him up against Woodward, McGeechan, Brian Ashton, Dean Richards, Fran Cotton, Jim Telfer or Andy Robinson, and he can match them all. Where I saw him at his best was his ability as a player to see a way through a problem during a match and take his team with him towards what always seemed like an inevitable conclusion. It was a rare skill.

Sadly it served him less well as the manager of the England team. Shorn of his match-day kit, dressed in a suit and tie, Johnson was deprived of his greatest asset. He was no longer one of the team, he was on the outside. Stranded in the dug-out he couldn't get out there and lead by example. Back at the hotel with the rest of the management, he couldn't be in the bars and put his arm around slumping shoulders and say 'you have had enough, let's get home'. He still showed the loyalty that mattered so much to us as players, but now, rather than cementing a team, it often highlighted his inexperience in the top job of an increasingly ruthless professional sport. Martin Johnson's biggest failing was the only thing he couldn't make up for with his sheer bloody-mindedness – a lack of experience.

Most other managers get to make mistakes on their way up, they learn their trade in the dark recesses of the game and only emerge into the spotlight when they have mastered their lines. Johnson's learning period was done in the full glare of the media and his mistakes shone out all the more as a result. It can't have been easy, and you could see how much the game and job consumed him. There was a stress on his face that never existed when he was a player. Never. Managing is as much politics as anything else and Machiavelli didn't write a guidebook because it came naturally to everyone. There were failings, and England at the World Cup were a disappointment. But should Johnno have gone? If he says the time has come then it has come.

I will back him in the same way that he always backed me, and I will not apologise for it. Yet when he talks of unfinished business I can't help but agree. This was a young side that was showing signs of promise. He was finding his feet as a manager and was improving. Yes, the team had messed up on a number of fronts in New Zealand, yet they could learn their lessons and be stronger for it. Just like their boss. I know there is no room for sentiment in professional sport, but when Martin Johnson resigned it was a sad day for English rugby.

The Greatest Tournament
Of Them All

The World Cup is the tournament I grew up dreaming of playing in. Even when there wasn't one, I used to pretend there was, basing it on football's version and picturing myself either scoring the try or dropping the goal that won it. When I got the chance to actually play in the final, I wasn't disappointed that my winning contribution was being pushed to the ground like a powder puff while Jonny Wilkinson kicked his now famous drop goal. It was a moment that I will never forget and it changed my life. For the new generations of rugby players growing up the World Cup is now the ultimate test, where the best teams from across the globe meet. The competition has continued to develop and grow since its first year in 1987 and its breadth and ambition is what makes it so special today. Where else would the minnows of world rugby get a chance every four years to take on the biggest fish? And while they may get taught a harsh lesson about playing rugby at the highest level it is still worthwhile. Their World Cup moments will revolve around the tackles they made on big-name stars, on the breaks they made through top-notch defences and the skills they showed while under the most intense pressure of their rugby careers. And while they may not get to lift the trophy, their memories of the World Cup will prove just as unforgettable as mine.

Have boots, will travel

As with most things in life, getting to do something is normally a disappointment when compared to how it was in your dreams. But not when you get your hands on the World Cup.

The hours I spent daydreaming about hoisting the Webb Ellis trophy above my head were nothing compared to the moment when I actually did it. Great big lumpy gold thing with pineapple-like growths and rams' horns all over it that would be ugly if it wasn't so damned precious.

Like the schoolyard bully's girlfriend – even though you know that getting your hands on her will cost you blood, sweat and plenty of tears, you don't care. You can't tear your gaze away and are drawn like a moth to a flame.

That's why I don't reckon too many players will be all that bothered about where the World Cup is played.

Sure everyone wants a comfy bed, a lovely pitch, and a nice pub to relax in after a tough game. But deep down, a player would turn out on a field of broken glass if it meant taking part in the greatest competition that the game has to offer.

As far as the players are concerned, I very much doubt that globalisation, finance, or sentimentality are the motivating factors that spring to mind. I am no Gareth Rees, a man who managed four World Cups, but I have been part of two and it is not the locations I remember, nor the stadiums, nor the bars.

What I remember are my team-mates, the banter, the defeats and the victories that I can recall as vividly as if they were yesterday.

Close my eyes and I am catching the Eurostar to Paris in 1999 for a quarter-final with South Africa, so full of hope, so excited about the biggest game of my life. Then suddenly the desolation of being stuffed, bitter laughs in the changing room with Phil de Glanville and Paul Grayson, and finally a night in the bars with Rowntree, Cockerill and Archer in full swing.

At the other end of the spectrum, training in Manly ahead of the 2003 semi-final and final, warming down with a swim in the sea and a bake in the Australian sun. Sitting on the bus with Johnson, Leonard and Dallaglio and looking into their eyes and knowing the semi-final was never going to be anything other than an English victory, no matter what the French brought to the party.

And finally, standing in the tunnel next to my centre partner and friend, Mike Tindall, and marvelling at the most enormous smile on his face as he revelled and sucked in the occasion of the final. These are the memories I will have of World Cups.

Would you prefer to have white clouds, high veldt, or cherry blossoms behind you when you lift the cup? I thought as much.

Australia 2003

More often than not it's only after an event that you realise how important it was. England's World Cup win in 2003 was the culmination of my personal rugby ambition. It was everything I had worked for and dreamt of. But when you are caught up in it, when you live it every day, you worry that it only matters that much to you, that it is your own personal obsession. What I have learnt since 2003 is that it meant an incredible amount to a huge number of people. I have lost count of the number of times I have been congratulated or someone has shared where they were and how they celebrated when we won. I have also been patted on the back and bought beers that I have happily supped with supporters. More than a few times, and by foreign supporters, I have been called lucky and a chancer. All of it is good, not least because it reminds me just how much rugby means to people and how closely intertwined all our memories and experiences of the highs and lows are.

This is why we play rugby

There is a knock on the dressing-room door. It's time to go. I am last out as always and Tinds [Mike Tindall] is in front of me. Stirling Mortlock and Elton Flatley are next to us and Tindall turns to them with a big smile and says in his broad Yorkshire accent: 'Now then, fellas, this is why we f***ing play rugby, isn't it? Listen to this noise. Let's get it on. Fantastic!' I look across and the two Australians are completely stony-faced. Are they nervous or do they just think Mike Tindall is a twit? Tindall's sheer joy gives me a big lift at any rate. He is right. This is bloody magnificent.

It starts and they score early on when Stephen Larkham puts up a perfectly executed cross-kick for Lote Tuqiri, who outjumps little Jason Robinson out on the wing. Flatley misses the conversion. Maybe he's thinking of Tindall. We get into the game, and start to find some rhythm. It feels good. Jonny [Wilkinson] slots two penalties and we are 6-5 up. The rain is still falling steadily, but we are throwing it around a bit. It is a massively physical encounter with huge hits all over the pitch.

There are 10 minutes to go before half-time when Ben Kay only has to fall over the line in the far corner to score, but the big idiot drops the ball for about the first time in a year. I can't believe it. I turn round to see Jonny lying motionless on the ground after putting in another massive tackle. It looks very, very bad and I'm standing there thinking: 'Get up, Wilko, come on, we need you.' He finally gets up and very soon he is slotting another penalty.

Tinds puts in a huge tackle on their captain George Gregan, lifting him off the ground and running him into touch. Then we get the try we deserve. From a line-out I take the ball into the midfield and get walloped by about four of them, but I manage to keep the ball in the ruck and squeeze it to Daws [Matt Dawson], who goes blind. [Lawrence] Dallaglio takes over and makes a storming run before offloading to Jonny, and I see Robinson flying up on his shoulder. No one is stopping Billy Whizz [Robinson] from here. Robbo bombs over at the corner and punches the ball into the air. The crowd are going potty.

Second half, and somehow they are back in it at 14-11 after Flatley bags a couple more penalties. These bloody Aussies don't know how to die. We are playing better than them but the points have dried up.

There are a few minutes to go and we are almost home when my moment of glory opens up before me. The ball is bobbling towards the Australian line and it's a straight race between me and Matt Rogers. If I can just get a boot to it, I'm in for a score no question, but Rogers slides in and beats me to it by inches. There are less than two minutes to go. I turn round to talk to Mike Tindall but he's not there. It's Mike Catt. What's he doing there? I see Tinds getting treatment on the touchline. The big fairy has got cramp.

There are seconds to go when the scrum collapses and the referee Andre Watson awards a penalty to Australia. Oh my giddy aunt. No way. I can really, really do without extra time. Flatley slots it. It's 14-14. 'How did that happen?' I'm wondering. Clive [Woodward] comes on to talk to us. Wilko cuts him off halfway through and says 'Woodie, sorry but I've got to go' and then runs off to practise his kicking. The rest of us go into a huddle. Nothing sophisticated or technical: 'Get the ball, keep it, run hard, give it everything, leave nothing on this field. Let's make sure we f***ing win it.'

Early in extra time we have a penalty after Johnno is taken out in the line-out. The boos are deafening as Jonny lines it up, but cool as ever he slots it and we are 17-14 up. The crowd start cranking out 'Swing Low'.

Everyone is going down with cramp and players seem to be coming and going. Iain Balshaw and Lewis 'Mad Dog' Moody are on the pitch. Who's gone off? There are about five minutes to go and I put in a massive tackle on Rogers and we get a penalty because he fails to release the ball. A minute later Watson is blowing up again and giving them a penalty in our half. What the fricking hell was that for? Flatley is under immense pressure again as he sets the ball up and prepares to kick. He does it again.

A minute or so before the critical moment of the entire tournament, and of our rugby careers, we have Australia almost back in their own 22-metre line when the ball is spun back to Rogers to clear.

Mad Dog takes off and launches himself at Rogers and the Aussie full-back half slices his kick into touch. We didn't know it right then, but in my view Mad Dog had just won us the World Cup.

There is about a minute or so to go, and we are looking at the nightmare of sudden death. Then it all happens very, very quickly. Steve Thompson launches a long throw to Moody at the back of the line-out and it is absolutely bang on the money. Mad Dog snaffles it and pops it to Daws. He feeds Catt who gets smashed, but looks after the ball. The ruck is formed and as Daws steps away from it to pass, Cockbain, their flanker, moves wide and creates a small gap and Daws is through it like a rat down a hole. He goes down in the tackle and I follow straight in to clean out the ball.

We are almost in drop-goal territory. Bang on cue arrives Johnno, Captain Marvel himself, who crashes forward and gains Jonny some extra yards and allows Daws to get up and feed the critical pass.

I'm in the ruck in front and the ball has to sail over my head to get to the posts. Daws has a quick look to get his bearings. He spins the ball back hard and flat to Jonny who drops it on to his right foot (his 'other' foot) and he lets fly. It's ugly and it's tumbling about all over the place in the air. But who bloody cares? The bugger's going through the sticks. Half the crowd is a happy red and white riot. The other is a sea of still gold. There's no real reaction from us at this point. There are about 30 seconds left on the clock. They've come back at us twice already and they could do it again unless we keep our heads.

They rush the restart and take it in the direction of their forwards when half of them aren't ready. Our prop Trevor Woodman catches it. At this point I find myself in the fly-half position next to Cattie with Wilko away somewhere on the other side of the pitch. It is essential Catt, who has a great kick, gets this next ball. So for the greatest moment in my rugby career and one of the very greatest moments in my life I go down on all fours like a dog and watch as Catt pummels the ball into row Z, triggering the biggest party in English sport for almost 40 years.

All I want to do is just jump up and down and hug somebody. I turn round and there is England's hero, Jonny Wilkinson, and we're hugging away with all the world's cameras trained on us and we're shouting 'World Cup! World Cup!' over and over again.

Champagne appears from somewhere. We set off on a lap of honour. The Australian Prime Minister, John Howard, then hands out all the medals very, very quickly and he barely stops to say anything to us as he whizzes along the line. Then it is time for Johnno to receive the Webb Ellis trophy.

We run around the pitch to parade the trophy, each taking it in turns to hold it aloft, and it is now, with the adrenalin from the match subsiding, that I notice that my shoulder is absolutely bloody agony.

France 2007

*The 2007 World Cup saw a very different England emerging.
Having changed managers twice in the four years between
competitions the team was a work in progress. Their style of
play was being criticised and questions were being asked about
the quality of the players that were getting picked. To many
observers English rugby was in danger of being left behind by
the powerful and exciting brand of the game that was being
played in the southern hemisphere and that would start to emerge
in countries such as Wales. As a result, very few of us expected
great things from an England side which eventually stunned
everyone by almost winning the final against South Africa.*

Balance is key for England

In the lead-up to the start of the 2006-07 season, alarm bells were being sounded regarding the state of the England team. My view was that there was no rush to condemn the team, especially when often the key to rugby success is making small changes that favour the long-term solution over the short-term fix.

Do you see yourself as one of life's sprinters or marathon runners? Do you jump out of the blocks in everything you do, take the early advantage and hope to hold on, or plan everything around an even pace knowing that come the end you will be in the mix as others struggle to maintain their early onslaught?

Each to their own. John Terry clearly likes the up-and-at-them bulldog style, while Kevin Pietersen won the Ashes on the final day with a method that resembled the Light Brigade. Me, I always preferred the softly, softly approach.

Maybe it was my sluggish pace and lack of muscle that saw me rely on a God-given talent for maintaining extreme levels of tedious organisation in the hope that the opposition would get fed up and go home.

Getting the balance right is tricky. So as the season begins today Andy Robinson and Rob Andrew, the Guinness Premiership clubs and any player with serious aspirations must all try to balance immediate success with long-term goals.

At national level, the dust may not have settled on the new coaching regime and its fresh-faced supremo but everyone is acutely aware of the importance of getting it right in November when the southern hemisphere invade.

There is absolutely, without doubt, no questions asked, plenty of time for England to mount a realistic challenge for the World Cup next year. What is absolutely crucial is that the new men in charge, without needing four wins out of four this autumn, manage to get a core group of 20 players together, one that will be enhanced by those who burst on to the scene and demand inclusion, just as Josh Lewsey did in 2003.

While it is true to say that England have been robbed of world-class young men in their prime, men like Phil Vickery, Trevor Woodman and Jonny Wilkinson, it is also fair to point out that in their absence mistakes have been made.

On occasion selection has been downright strange, and players have added to the mayhem with less than clever decisions. But among the problems there have been signs that the coaching staff are getting their point across and the players are understanding and adapting.

Victory against New Zealand is almost irrelevant. What must be avoided, however, is indecision because while a sprint would help, a more measured, controlled approach is just as important.

At club level needs are different. Ignore the cliche about not winning trophies at Christmas, it is merely a coaches' ploy to keep players' feet on the ground and alleviate pressure. Get caught in the blocks and the Premiership trap door begins to creak very quickly, even before the Heineken Cup comes rushing up a mere six weeks into the new season.

Bristol showed us last year that against all odds a good start can propel a team to things never thought possible. Confidence in a club side is priceless. Get a bad start and the rot rushes in and begins to demoralise an entire club.

Managing a squad is vital, but rotating players, giving talent a chance, keeping things fresh and trying the unexpected, these are the sweet luxuries that come only with early success.

Forget the 100-yard dash and long-distance grind, if anything the opening weekend of the Premiership is like the start of a triathlon. From a standing start, the competitors head for the open water in a wild thrash of energy, a mass of rippling muscle, low body fat and incredible aerobic capacity. Forget style, forget elegance, leave aesthetics in the changing room, just find some space and bloody win.

As for the top-class, elite players, it is a juggling act. Glory with a club can equal almost any achievement with the national team. The players are your best friends, the supporters are your biggest fans. And with many lads still turning out for local teams, hearing the Saturday whistle in club colours would have been something they dreamt of as they grew up.

As good as it gets, however, players will still have their eye on the ultimate prize, for nothing whatsoever could equal the feeling of standing in a stadium packed with England fans, a gold medal around your neck.

So the players will come out this weekend, their bodies pulsing with adrenalin, trying to keep their heads ice-cold, trusting in their skills. They will have muttered to themselves to be brave in the tackle, committed at the ruck, and to think clearly in the middle of the mayhem.

They will pray to make the right decisions, and find the gaps that let them break away from the pack, running as fast as their legs will carry them, hoping beyond hope that club and country will help them get to the goal line even quicker.

May the force be with him

Brian Ashton is wrong! There, I've said it. It stuck in my throat, and I half expected secret agent thugs to come bursting through the door, slamming me to the ground and gagging me before I could get the words out.

You see, Brian has become the oracle, the sage of rugby, and I, one of his favourite pupils, have dared to question him. But he'll love it. Brian doesn't like lemmings – he likes people who question the status quo, he loves challenges, and being in charge of England's attack in the lead-up to France 2007 is about as big a challenge as you can get.

Brian looked after me on a rugby field from a very early age, he and my dad enjoying a mid-Seventies jaunt to Italy. In Rome, he was a diminutive, uber-skilful scrum-half, part coach and part babysitter to me, a two-year-old Roman street urchin. After a year he headed up to Milan, where his coaching developed as quickly as his ability to gather nicknames. This is the man whom we initially called Ernie (after Bert and Ernie in *Sesame Street*), who then matured into Yoda due to his deep-seated knowledge and mystical mastery of the game.

Yet it was in Milan that he gained his best nom de plume. Paired with another follically challenged half-back, Dave Cornwall, they became known as *i pellati* – the peeled ones. Returning to the UK with a wealth of experience but sadly no more hair, Brian continued his coaching studies at Stonyhurst, a Jesuit priest-run school that was my alma mater and the sworn enemies of Lawrence Dallaglio's Benedictine monks at Ampleforth.

The school days have been left behind, and Brian has gone from strength to strength. He played a leading role in helping to develop England's game at the start of the millennium, and it was a pleasure to be around such a free thinker. Anyone who believes we won the World Cup by smashing it up the middle needs a mallet to the head.

We played different styles of rugby, sometimes changing mid-season, sometimes changing mid-match. This came not only from having an attack coach who wanted players to express themselves, but also from having the players who understood when to play and when to batten down the hatches. And this is where Brian and I are at loggerheads, because the wise one does not believe our top players have the skills to win at the highest levels.

Brian does not believe that their skills are good enough to stand up to the extraordinary levels of pressure in today's Test matches. I believe that the ability of our players is as good as, if not better than, the squad that won a World Cup. The problem England have is not a lack of skills, it is a lack of understanding. In a nutshell, they don't know when to pass, when to kick and when to run.

If this sounds worrying, it is. And it raises two big questions. Firstly, how do you go about addressing the problem across the Premiership as a whole? And secondly, how do you fix it in time to mount a realistic challenge for next year's World Cup?

Long-term development versus short-term sticking plaster. Let's take a look at the long-term options first. One of the main factors has been an over-reliance on the bench-press and other manly gym exercises. In our desire to address the physical side of rugby, we have forgotten that the brain is the biggest muscle in the body. Develop that, and you have a chance of producing world-beating rugby players. Fail to stimulate it and all you get are gym-honed battering rams that quickly and powerfully disappear up their own dead ends.

Whatever happened to the subtle arts of game management and understanding? Instead of turning a new page, our academies are teaching by the book. Practice may make perfect, but it is a poor substitute for game time. Too many of our best players are snapped up straight from school, paid a few quid, lobbed into an academy and given the occasional game in the 'A' league. This is not enough to develop and nurture world-class talent in depth.

Game time is everything for a young player. In a live game, if you make the wrong decision you pay for it. You don't learn to play in a gym and in practice; you do it in games, twice a week, come hell or high water.

So how do England fix the problem within a year? With great difficulty is the simple answer. But bringing in Brian Ashton, a guy who understands the game better than any Englishman in the last decade, is a bloody good start. Brian does not preach rocket science; he seeks understanding, a forum for debate and the freedom for players to get on and win the game their way. There is no faking it with Yoda – if you are a lightweight he will spot you a mile away.

Senior players be warned. He is very, very good at what he does. Let's just hope the force is with him and he has enough time to turn English rugby away from the dark side.

Believe in the unbelievable

Shock the world – STW. That phrase and those three letters are all over the England changing rooms at the moment.

The players got their first glimpse of the powerful message before the matches against Wales and France in August. Huge signs were hanging everywhere. You can understand why the management have done it.

England have been written off by almost everyone. Even the most optimistic of mums must be struggling to believe that her little boy can go on to ultimate glory in the World Cup.

Over the past four years, the national team have stumbled from game to game, never getting into a rhythm that would get supporters' hearts pounding. Occasionally, Twickenham was set alight, only for England to lose matches at home that they should have won, and then go on the road and wilt under the onslaught of foreign aggression.

The world? It doesn't even come close but you've got to love the belief.

One certainty is that by the time kick-off comes tonight, England's players will be breathing a collective sigh of relief. The worst part of a World Cup is the waiting, all four years of it.

Pundits give their views on everything from the team's age to their choice of kit. Should we build for this tournament or the next? Focus on 2007 or 2011? Round and round in circles, like a dog chasing its tail, the press pack has chewed over every bone like it was filet mignon.

Coaches have come and gone, players have changed from week

to week. Bravery has not been enough because sport is all about winning.

Ever since the final whistle went at the Stade Velodrome in Marseille three weeks ago, it has been one long wait for all these players. Press conference after press conference, trying to toe the party line. Send-off dinners surrounded by well-wishers and autograph hunters. Question after question straight batted back – 'Yes we can win', 'it will be very tough but we believe in what we are doing', 'whoever Brian picks at No 8 will be top class on the night', 'New Zealand are the team to beat'.

On and on the sound bites go. For some, it is not a chore, they do it with a smile, understanding the importance of the supporter and the sponsor, not just now but in the future. Others try to hide away, they cannot leave dinners fast enough. On occasion they may be rude, but since when were all rugby players cut from the same cloth?

Now all that is over, the talking is done. Over the next six weeks, England and its players will find out exactly where they stand in the world rankings.

There will be no way to shy away from the truth. World Cup records speak for themselves and hang like a millstone around the necks of the successful and failures for a long time. For the players, the days of reckoning have come.

They realise that they are the lucky ones, they understand the enormity of the task ahead of them, and they will not shirk in their attempts to live up to the expectations of a nation. All they ask in return is that we on the touchlines and on the sofa at home give them our support.

An international team is never made up of the 15 players who are the best in the world in their position. You will have some world-beaters and some nearly-men. Players understand this, as do coaches. They will make the decisions they believe to be the right ones on the pitch, and the backroom staff will try to pick a team they believe will give England the best chance of winning.

The one thing that they can do nothing about, however, is how the crowd reacts – and it can make all the difference.

So if you are lucky enough to find yourself in the stadium this evening, and over the coming weeks, make yourself heard. Never underestimate your power as a supporter.

When the team comes under pressure, should they go behind on points, or be reduced to 14 or even 13 men through indiscretion and find themselves besieged on their own line, then raise your voices even louder.

You can make the difference. I only ever knew the English crowd as magnificent – make sure you are never anything less. Back home it is no different, and the impact can be even more potent. If a vibe of belief begins to grow do not think the players won't hear about it. Press officers cut out all the articles and photocopy them for players to read at breakfast. Get positive, and the news will go hurtling across the English Channel.

We will be talking about the next World Cup soon enough. For now enjoy English rugby, support your team, and believe we can do it all over again. If the players believe they can Shock The World, then for six weeks so must we.

The battle against South Africa

The most revealing aspect of England's game against the United States came after the final whistle. It was not the mortuary-like state of the England changing room. Nor the defensive answers in the press conference – they are par for the course after a poor performance. No, it happened out on the pitch where England had struggled to prove themselves worthy of the title 'world champions'.

Ten minutes after the final whistle, the substitutes came out to run around and get the blood pumping; dirt tracking, as it is known. The bench boys have adrenalin coursing through their veins but it has not had an outlet. They want to feel involved. Martin Corry, Matt Stevens and Andy Farrell were out there. They had only played about 20 minutes of real game time. But there was someone else with them.

Smiling, in among it, enjoying himself, was Jamie Noon. I will just let that sink in – Jamie Noon. He had just played a full Test match for England in a World Cup, and yet there was something he wanted to get out of his system. As happy as I was to see Jamie enjoying himself, it is a sad indictment of where England find themselves if their starting centre is so excluded from a Test match that he has to go out and play a game after a game. And he is not alone in a team full of mixed emotions.

There is anger, frustration, a lack of enjoyment. England have been down in the dumps for too long. Tonight they have to perk themselves up, find a performance to be proud of and try to match a team, South Africa, who seem to be doing a lot right.

Both sides came under pressure last weekend. One responded in slow motion, the other absorbed the pressure, looked for outlets, varied their play, refused to be bullied and found a way to release their attacking weapons. And what an arsenal it is.

South Africa have physicality bordering on brutality. Their line-out is world class, the scrum would do well against a giant steamroller, and they are pulling off back moves straight out of the old-school playbook. Out wide they have a winger who has to be the first name written into any World XV team-sheet right now – Bryan Habana.

South Africa are a team becoming increasingly comfortable with attacking variations. At their core, backs' moves or team moves are all about scoring a try. But they can also ask questions of a defence, even if they do not break through first time. They help sow seeds of indecision, they get the other guys thinking about what they are doing. Think too much and you may not react quickly enough, creating tiny gaps and opportunities that allow a player and team to win the battle to get over the gain line.

Keep chipping away, chopping things up, and instead of hard-hitting shoulders making the tackles, it suddenly becomes desperate wrists and flailing arms. The opposition cannot get into good positions because elements of guesswork have started to appear in their defensive systems.

So where does that leave England tonight? Up against it would be a kind way of putting it. England cannot reinvent the wheel in a week but there are tactical changes that would help them still be in the game after 60 minutes. Numbers one to five have to come out of the changing room climbing the walls. They have to scrum with every ounce, win line-out ball and smack anything in a green shirt. This is old-fashioned but sensible.

They have to stand toe-to-toe with 'Bakkies' Botha and his

cohorts, and they have to come off knowing they are spent and have gone to war.

The back row must swarm, snaffle, pilfer, shift the ball away from contact, and tackle, tackle, tackle. Occasionally they might be allowed into the open spaces as ball carriers. Then they must make the right decision between kicking down the door, and offloading and supporting the backs.

Numbers nine and 10 must dictate, make decisions and back them. Former Australia and Leicester coach Bob Dwyer still believes there is no such thing as a bad rugby decision, only one that is not carried through with conviction. Make the call and stand by it. Give England a lead, kick well, understand when to run and when simply to get it out of danger. Vary the style of play. You have a playbook, use it. Never look as though you don't know what you are doing. Panic spreads quickly through a team, as France found to their cost.

Centres, when your fly-half asks you to make some tough yards, do not question why. Use your feet and if there is a wall in front of you, win that contact. Look forward to the wide play being called and when it is, you must pass as if your very existence depends on it. Run accurate decoy lines, and turn every kick into a good one by closing down space.

For the back three, positional play is crucial. Do not allow opposition kicks to bounce, do not dither at the back, defend your line with everything you have and give your fly-half options in attack. Communicate space and be patient. If you are outnumbered, stay with Habana and hope the other, slower South Africans are caught.

Remember the motto that no ball is given away cheaply and every yard is earned. Whatever happens tonight, not a single England player can come off the field and fancy a quick game of touch.

A difficult evening

Rugby is a sport that borrows heavily from the language of war. Teams fight for territory and players go into battle. The World Cup is a campaign and coaches talk of sacrifice for a band of brothers. Unfortunately England's attempt to retain their title is far from the blitzkrieg that many of us had hoped for.

Against South Africa we were shown just how dangerous it can be to put your faith in big, slow-moving units when the opposition are buzzing around like guerilla fighters. A moving target is much harder to hit, and the Springboks made sure that England were always a yard or two off the pace. Key to their success was the scrum-half Fourie du Preez, and his performance summed up the difference between the two sides.

He was sensational, and proved just as destructive as Jonah Lomu and his four-try romp in the semi-final of 1995. Du Preez was quicker in deed and mind than anyone else on the field. From a maul in his own half, he saw the faintest of dog-legs in the England defence, lured his opposite number Shaun Perry and then moved the ball to his winger when the England man lunged forward. Playground stuff.

Du Preez then tracked the winger's run with the grace of a cheetah, picked up the inside ball, stepped and half-broke Jason Robinson's tackle, using a powerful leg drive to get back on his feet. He then ignored his first wave of support players because he knew they were attacking a channel where England's cover tacklers could get them and dragged the ball back 10 yards to the rampaging Juan Smith, who had a clear run to the line. The move had vision, tenacity, daring, speed, power and skill.

When South Africa won a penalty he backed himself and put in a pinpoint cross-field kick that only just saw Jacque Fourie fail to dot down a certain seven pointer.

In the first half, England had a chance to score from a loose pass from the South African ruck as Andy Farrell tried to hack forward. But Du Preez seized the ball, spun, outstripped the first defender on his inside, veered out, ran away from the cover, drew Robinson and gave JP Pietersen a canter home.

And if you want proof that he is cunning, just look at how he won a penalty and three points by running into Matt Stevens at a ruck. Smart, quick and inventive – three words that would not pop up when talking about England.

The team were smashed in the tackle – head-jarring hits every time England looked to be aggressive. As a result they had to commit so many numbers to the breakdown that it limited the options in attack. South Africa's back three could just sit back and wait for counter-attacking opportunities.

This goes some way to explaining why England had no cutting edge. The backs shuffled sideways and never looked like scoring. Wherever England turned they met South Africans because at no point did they break up their defensive patterns or make them think. Ask yourself if Percy Montgomery, the South African full-back, ever had to make a one-on-one tackle? I think you can work out the answer.

England's restarts and 22 kick-offs were long and never gave the players a chance to regather possession. Their turnovers were into double figures, putting the team on the back foot and allowing South Africa to dominate the contact. England gave away too many free kicks and penalties early on, handing over the initiative and blowing their plan of containment out of the water.

If you want to strangle a game, you need to have near-perfect execution and defensive concentration. Instead, England were on the back foot from the outset.

It was a difficult evening. Even so, there was a handful of positives. The scrum was solid and England took ball against the feed. Andrew Sheridan did his job and it was good to see him get some yards with the ball in his hands. Nick Easter got better as the game went on.

Robinson was making it past tacklers before his hamstring let him down. He told me after the game, cotton wool stitched into his eyelid, dried blood all over his face and shirt, leg wrapped in ice, that he was a quick healer. Reckons that he has age on his side, his dry wit still as sharp as his angles of run. The guy is an inspiration and if England are to progress in the World Cup, then the players need to take a page out of his book.

Winston Churchill once said that success is going from failure to failure without losing your enthusiasm. The next week will show how hungry this England team is for success and whether or not they have the stomach for a fight.

Crunch time for England

I was going to send the England team a good luck message before the South Africa game but the spectre of spellcheck made me drop my phone. The plan was to say 'have a blinder' but it kept getting changed to 'blunder'. Little did I know how accurate it would prove to be.

I have been too scared to send anything this week because England are on the brink of sporting catastrophe, in danger of turning from champs to chumps. It shows the state of panic among the nation's supporters that we have doubts about England's ability to beat Samoa – who lost to Northampton and Harlequins in their World Cup warm-up fixtures.

Pre-tournament, today's game would have been viewed as a physical fixture in which the biggest worry was getting through without injuries. Now we fear a mortal wound to England's rugby honour.

Make no mistake, for many involved with the England team this coming week is do or die. Defeat by the Samoans and an exit at the group stage, whether today or after the Tonga game on Friday, would end careers; players, coaches and Rugby Football Union management alike could not survive a sporting disaster of such magnitude.

England's two performances have lacked any authority, wit, flair, dynamism, nastiness or precision. Tactics have been poor, style non-existent. The tempo has been so staccato that it has stalled. Brains have not been engaged enough to implement a change of tack.

Nor have they been switched off enough for the players to ignore pain and lose themselves in a defensive frenzy. Stuck in a zombie-like state, they seem unable to do anything other than watch their World Cup unravel.

Eddie Jones – the Australian coach who has opened South African eyes to a world beyond contact and unleashed the speed and talent of players such as Schalk Burger, Fourie du Preez, Bryan Habana and Jaque Fourie – has talked of northern hemisphere rugby becoming 'stodgy'. He is right and what worries me is that our game has become so heavy and tasteless that the players have completely lost their appetite.

I was in Bordeaux last Saturday for one of the great big-game atmospheres as the Georgians came so close to a famous victory against the shell-shocked Irish. Held up on the line, the Georgians were denied the biggest World Cup upset only by a thin Irish wall that would have succumbed had the game gone on any longer. At the end, the stadium rose as one to salute true gladiators from the Caucasus.

The Samoans will have watched this and taken heart, reckoning that another smaller nation is due an upset. They will also be fighting for their tournament lives, having lost to Tonga. England must find their big-match composure fast.

Selection was going to be key and for me they needed to be brave. They have tried experience without pace, now it seems England want to try pace with inexperience. Good, it cannot go any worse and even if players such as Mathew Tait and Olly Barkley do not have all that many caps between them, they do have enough nous to make a go of it.

England's front five must maintain their good work in the scrum, one of the few positives to emerge from the gloom of Paris. They must force the Samoan pack to focus on set-piece work. If England do not punish Samoa physically in the tight, they will roam free and punch holes across the field.

Defence must be watertight in technique. My teachers used to love telling me that the bigger someone was, the harder they would fall. It was absolute rubbish. The bigger they are the more it hurts, but pain can be no excuse today.

Discipline will also be crucial, as will precision and accuracy of pass. Poor handling sank Wales against Australia and showed just how big the gap now is between the hemispheres.

Wales' James Hook missed his full-back with a pass and put the team under pressure. By contrast, and in the next couple of plays, Australia's Matt Giteau fired a pinpoint delivery into the space in front of Drew Mitchell. Stride was not broken, pace was maintained, the last tackle was taken in control, and the ball was popped inside to the grateful Chris Latham. Glorious. Pass to the space, invite your friends forward, and have sympathy with the weight of ball.

When watching Six Nations teams this World Cup, too often instead of seeing buzzing feet and hands, you hear the dull thud of the ball on the chest of the recipient. With it goes any hope of momentum and quick ball.

England are hanging on by their fingertips – and they need to use them to stay in the World Cup. Fail and the next text message I send will not be 'what a band of winners'. I hate to think what spellcheck might make of that.

Now for the pressure cooker

The knockout stages of a World Cup are a cold and ruthless place. In the group games there is an element of enjoyment, and a safety net that can allow teams to lose a match and still progress. The atmosphere is decidedly festival as household names come face to face with the amateur stalwarts that keep the Corinthian spirit of our game alive.

But overnight all this comes to an end. The smiles disappear and the frowns become deeper. It is time to concentrate because from here on in there are no second chances – you either perform or you head home.

In 2003, England saw how easy it was to get it wrong and just how fast things can turn against you. I knew we were in trouble when the Brisbane stadium was alive with the chants of 'Wales, Wales', and there were daffodils and leeks everywhere.

We were chasing shadows, and we just could not get hold of the ball. The scoreboard showed us two tries to nil down and our legs were beginning to go. The half-time whistle could not come soon enough.

Remember those old Westerns on a Sunday afternoon, when the hero faces a certain death but still goes out there to face down his black-hatted nemesis, trusting his ice-cold nerves? Well, it's a pretty similar feeling when things are going badly for you on a rugby field.

And you had better get used to it because I don't care who you are – and this includes the unstoppable All Blacks – you will come under pressure in the knockout stages of the World Cup. How you deal with it will determine whether you keep going through the tournament.

Just look at the Wales Fiji match, swinging from one side to the next, from one up to one down. In the end it was about split-second decisions taken in the dying moments of a game.

The key to success is building your belief, to understand what you are doing, to keep going when at times it may seem you have no chance of winning.

Teams must react and cope with going behind. In 2003, England fell behind in all the knockout games. Stay together, and you have a chance. New Zealand in 1999 and the French in 2003 both crumbled when the squeeze came on. The Aussies know how to manage a game, keep it going and grind it out.

At this stage of the World Cup, all it needs is for one guy to wilt under pressure, to start doing things that have not been worked through on the training field, and the wheels can suddenly come off. It is not just the weaker teams who crack under pressure, the best ones do as well. Start making problems for your team, and the opposition gain in confidence.

Players need to be comfortable with what they are doing and that comes only with practice and repetition. In 2003, England's attention to detail was unrivalled. We practised what to do if we had two players in the sin-bin at the same time, luck had nothing to do with it. How many other teams went into so much detail?

This time around, the others have caught up, and you can bet that Graham Henry, Jake White and the others will not be leaving anything to chance. The players will be waving goodbye to continental beers and late nights, if they have not already done so.

Unfortunately, in the knockout stages you become something of a rugby-playing monk and an anti-social arse. You know that one of your matches will come down to the final five minutes and you have to be ready.

Your body becomes a temple, and you look after everything making sure there are no niggles, no slight aches or pains. An hour a day is spent with the masseur and physio.

You only get one crack at it and you have to be able to look at yourself in the mirror and say 'I could not have done anything differently'. If you lose and wish you could have changed things, then you will have failed.

This eye to detail, this management of time and people is at the heart of what happens both on and off the field.

And while consistency is vital off the park, variety is the winner on it. The successful team will have to know how to chop and change, and break up the game. They will have to gain an understanding of the ebb and flow of a match, quickly getting a feeling for what is going on and they will have to be able to box clever.

Towards the end of the first half against Australia at the last World Cup, Jonny Wilkinson went down and everyone held their breath. Martin Johnson sensed the situation and gathered the team around him. 'Don't look at him!' he screamed. 'We will win this game whether he plays or not!' A brilliant load of rubbish if ever I heard it, but it had the right effect. The forwards looked at each other and grunted in agreement, chests puffed up with pride and determination. One of Johnno's main strengths was his ability to react to pressure and say the right things.

Clarity and chaos, that is what the knock out stages are all about. The teams that can best see a way through the blinding fog of fear and anticipation are the ones that will keep moving towards their ultimate prize.

Dreams can come true

The Georgian and George – two people whose words have captured my imagination and who may hold the key to England beating Australia. First up is the Georgian loosehead prop, Mamuka Magrakvelidze. Turns out he is a big man with a poet's heart. 'Sport is where dreams come true,' he says. Never has a truer word been spoken and it is exactly what England must hope for this weekend.

If they had to play Australia 10 times in 10 weeks, the Aussies would win nine. But they would lose once, and England have to hope that their victory is due at Stade Velodrome in Marseille this afternoon. The only problem they have is that George Gregan is standing in the way. I was looking through some old paper cuttings this week and chanced upon a Gregan quote spoken in the aftermath of that game four years ago when he was mulling over his future. 'I'm going to take pleasure in unpacking my bags, chilling out and then make a decision.' Well, decide he did, and George kept on going.

There are several things to consider here, most importantly what drove a man on for a further four years? It was not hatred, it was not revenge. Rather it was about finishing his career at the appropriate moment and that night four years ago was not it for the little man. So here he is again lining up against England plotting, planning and talking, always talking.

His head is shinier than ever, shorts as clean at the end of the game as they are at the start. A gentleman off the field, he does so much charity work that it would put some of the most ardent philanthropists to shame. A devoted family man he may be, but cross the lines of a rugby field and he turns into a born winner.

Never a backward step, he is always cajoling, probing, sledging. Not a word commonly used in rugby, sledging, mainly because you do not have the time to think of clever comments while someone is trying to knock your block off. But George does, and who can forget the semi-final four years ago when Australia were seconds away from dumping New Zealand, their old rivals from across the Tasman Sea, out of the tournament. George was in Byron Kelleher's face, taunting his opposite number, shouting 'four more years, boys, four more years!' Harsh, but then you need an edge if you are going to win hundreds of caps. Nothing is a lost cause; the match is always there to be won.

Look at his tackle on Jeff Wilson in a Bledisloe Cup that happened so long ago it might as well have been in black and white.

Wilson, one of the game's supreme finishers and a New Zealand great, was in mid-air, on the way to scoring the match-winning try. George hit him so hard and so perfectly in the sweet spot that the ball was dislodged from the flying winger's hands and Australia, instead of losing, ended up doing the All Blacks again.

This World Cup finally signals the end of Gregan's majestic career and he will not want to go down to the English again. He won't want to lose to the Kiwis, or South Africans. In fact I don't believe he is thinking about losing at all. What he wants to do for one last time is pull the strings, shape the team's play, dictate the rhythm and tempo of the match, and steer Australia to the ultimate prize.

That's what he does so beautifully, and if England want to have any hope of winning they have to stop him, get him dirty. Let him stroll around, deliver his passes, nurdle his kicks, and it is over. This is easier said than done. Gregan has played behind packs who look as if they are on roller skates they are going backwards so quickly. Yet he still drives them to victory.

At the same time, George is not easy to get hold of, running around so daintily that he looks like a butterfly with sore feet. Better teams than England have tried and failed to neutralise this nugget of chatting gold. A tough ask, though not impossible.

What England must do is focus on the breakdowns. They have to be turned into a bun fight, and Argentina gave a master-class of how it should be done against Ireland. Whether individually or in a group, England's technique must be good, staying low and on their feet.

England's line-out must function and they must put pressure on Australia because the Wallabies launch a lot of moves off the back with a long throw. This allows Gregan to either execute run-around plays and deliver pinpoint passes, or peel around the back and have a run himself, bringing other players into the charge. England have to starve him of possession and then close him down.

One weakness for Australia is the scrum. They might be better than in 2005, when they lost 26-16 at Twickenham, but they are still not the world's best. England must attack at every scrum, make it difficult at the base and not give Gregan a solid platform from which to snipe and launch his very dangerous back line. England need to drag him into everything, legally of course, and hold him down, not so legally. They also need to follow through with their tackles. I mean this in a nice way. When you are in the process of tackling certain players and they pass the ball, it is often best to pull out, to stop immediately, and go on to help out at the next one. George is not one of those players. If you are mid-tackle and he gets the ball away, finish off what you were doing. Remember Mike Tindall's hit?

You have to slow up and break down Australia's link between classy openside flanker George Smith and Berrick Barnes, the new lad at fly-half. Barnes looks world class given time and I am sure he will go on to be another Wallaby cracker, but he will not have played in a game like this before. Limit the quality of his possession and Barnes will have an uncomfortable afternoon, even with Matt Giteau and Stirling Mortlock looking after him.

That is what today is about for England – making it uncomfortable for Australia. The Wallabies are a wonderfully incisive team who can live off scraps if needs be and have become the ultimate unpickers of defences. Yet England still have a chance.

As my Georgian friend points out, dreams can come true. But so can nightmares, and England have to give George Gregan a match that will chase away sleep and have him breaking out in a cold sweat for years to come. Stop the scrum-half today and England stop the green and gold of Australia.

England find their hard edge

Anyone wanting a better understanding of how England produced a match of such industrial precision against Australia need only look at the team's hotel. Set near the stadium in downtown Marseille, it did not have the views of the ocean that greeted the South Africans and others each morning. Instead of tranquillity, it had city noise and swirl.

In the knockout stages, matches become a lottery, but then so does the accommodation, locations drawn out of a hat. For England, who moved in after the Georgians headed home, the rough edges would have only served to remind them how far they had fallen, and how completely Lady Luck had turned her back. Funny then such ugly surroundings could have conjured up such beauty, both in image and deed.

I do not know which moment sticks more in my mind. Whether it was the New Zealand fan, who earlier had brought the house down with his impromptu Haka in a Marseille bar, sinking into his seat as the French stole his dream, or the sight of George Smith, Australia's match-winner over so many years, slipping silently from the field of play with a quarter of the game to go. It might be the pandemonium in Marseille as English and French fans kissed and hugged each other firstly from the joy of victory, and then in the realisation that the best of old enemies would be facing each other in the semi-final.

But if I am honest, there is one image that best sums up what surely must have been the craziest Saturday in international sport there has been. Standing alone in the tunnel of the stadium, a bespectacled Brian Ashton texts away on his phone, getting in touch with his pals, his kids or someone up there, trying to make sense of it all.

After all the madness, there he was fixed in normality, doing the everyday thing, a reminder that England's game against Australia had actually started to script. There was a long English kick-off to start the game, a great take by Stirling Mortlock, a comfortable ruck for George Gregan, a beautiful pass to Chris Latham and a massive clearance kick putting England back in their own half. Effortless, classy, what we were expecting from Australia. Then everything gets turned on its head.

To see Peter Richards giving Gregan the verbals during his brief cameo told you all you needed to know about the England mood. If you wanted further proof, then how about Nick Easter tapping the ball on Dan Vickerman's head and calling him a naughty boy for conceding another penalty.

These were not empty words nor threats. Instead they reflected a confident attitude that was built on a rock-solid foundation of hard graft, determination, bloody-mindedness and a ferocity of intensity that the Australians could do nothing about.

The Wallabies manufactured one well-worked try when they were allowed to go through the phases. Yet instead of folding like an Australian front-row forward, England stepped up the gears in their counter-rucking. England knew that the Australians liked to form one-man rucks in order to get the ball to the floor quickly, roll it away to Smith who would feed Gregan and he, in turn, would get the backs moving. This is how Australia like to play, it lets them move teams around and find gaps, and it lets them move on to the ball on the gain line.

Not on Saturday. Giant feet and huge English shoulders battered every ruck, refused to allow the Australians to get the ball up and away, and dragged Gregan into the bun fight he didn't want to get involved in. Berrick Barnes may be a great player in the making but England were not going to let him find out. Lewis Moody had one of those games. He was everywhere, marauding, hassling, chasing lost causes. Mike Catt will need a week-long ice bath to give him a chance of playing next week, a battered picture of how much England gave for this win.

Yet none of the heroics would have mattered if it had not been for the men up front. Andrew Sheridan was a one-man wrecking machine. He had a total game. His ball-carries took three Australians to bring him down. He smashed into rucks and mauls, draining the Australians' energy levels every time he released his body into action. Simply awesome and the world sat up and took notice of a big man who lets his actions do the talking.

Supported by his trusty pals Mark Regan and Phil Vickery, who were replaced by the equally effective George Chuter and Matt Stevens, the scrum was a sight to behold. It squeezed the life from the Australians and left them without a platform.

There has been a change of mindset in the England team, and it cannot have been a coincidence that Sheridan had his best game against a team he has already demolished.

It makes a difference when you look across a front row and see players you have taken to the cleaners. In rugby, familiarity does not breed contempt, but it certainly lets you break down the opposition in your mind, and it gives you the extra ounce of power needed to win matches at the highest level.

When England face France, the players will not be strangers. Many of them are from the same clubs, others will have played each other in European competition. England will have to try to bottle whatever it was that made them so fearsome on Saturday and uncork it at just the right moment.

I just hope that moving to the opulence of Versailles does not turn their hard edge soft.

Bon courage!

The French do cool better than the English. We may have the pop music, but they can do something simple and it captures the moment. A plume of cigarette smoke, a shrug of the shoulders. Take the final seconds of their quarter-final against New Zealand.

Under immense pressure, they refused to buckle as the All Blacks kept coming. Then, amid one final, desperate push, New Zealand spilled the ball and it ended up in the hands of one Jean-Baptiste Elissalde. Also called the Rat, this scrum-half is a sportsman who knows when his time has arrived.

The clock had run down, the ball simply had to go out and France were through to the semi-finals, a nation's hopes re-ignited by the valour of their gladiators. Lesser men would have hammered the ball into touch. Get it over quickly. Not Jean-Baptiste, he is too bloody clever.

Some players look as though they have time on the ball, but there are others who see things five phases ahead of everyone else, those who make the whole confrontational shooting match look like a stroll in the park. The Rat is one of the latter, and there was no fear for him that it would end badly, no worry that he would make an error that might kill victory. Elissalde was not going to let the opportunity pass to enjoy himself. There was nothing disrespectful in his actions, yet while he had no intention of taunting the New Zealanders he would be damned if he did not enjoy every last second.

So it was that he set off across the field sideways. Forrest Gump-style, he just ran until he ran out of pitch, punting the ball away, bringing the game to an end and the stadium to its feet. All the way he had been smiling, not wanting the moment to end.

It summed up everything that is good about sport – when a player has beaten his demons and conquered tension. Elissalde was totally relaxed and in control of his own destiny. He was loving every second of it. But for each moment of joy there also comes pain, and the flip side of knockout stages can be just as absorbing. The previous day I had watched with dark fascination as Australia's Matt Giteau stood outside his team huddle alone, staring at the English side who had just upset the odds so dramatically and dumped the Wallabies out of the competition. Giteau is a great player – do not let any performance persuade you otherwise – and there he was like a green and gold zombie.

He stared at the England players and their celebrations, taking in the moment as it unfolded. Giteau was watching and locking away the images in a corner of his mind where they will stay until he is next in a fight for survival. Then they will be conjured up to drive him on through the tough times, because there is no way he will ever want to feel like that again. As painful as it was, Giteau would not avert his eyes. I admired him for doing it, and he will be a better player for it.

Both France and England have suffered in this tournament. They lost early games and fought back to bring about the most unlikely of semi-finals. But they have also enjoyed the headiest of times. On Saturday we will see which has left the most lasting impression.

The players must summon up their courage and wear it like armour. In the pack, it will be brutal. France are bigger and nastier than the Australians and will make England pay should the boys in white slip in their intensity. The scrummage will again be key, a signal of intent from the outset. At the line-out, England will have to dominate if they want to suffocate the French and try to rattle their cage. Let Les Bleus run and pass at pace and England will find it difficult to shut them out. Get on top of them, get in their faces, break up their rhythm and France have proven to be fragile.

The irony is that in this most ugly of confrontations, the team who keep their inner smile may be the ones who triumph. England's three-quarters, subdued in so many previous matches, suddenly found their vim against Australia. France are the masters of flowing rugby, and yet have proved fractious in recent weeks, running up dead ends and sputtering to a halt when they most needed to accelerate away.

Players on both sides will have to back themselves and their team-mates to make the break, to pass into space and to get over the tryline. They will have to have the guts to seize the moment. It only takes a second to get it right. Get it wrong and four years will seem like forever.

Making the impossible possible

In the lead-up to Saturday's match-winning dropped kick, Jonny Wilkinson looked like he had lost his mind. The forwards were driving the ball up, recycling it and trying to get the extra inches that could make all the difference.

Wilkinson, meanwhile, was pacing left to right, forwards, backwards, looking down and looking up. This is it, I thought, he's finally gone gaga under the pressure.

Then the penny dropped. Surrounded by semi-final madness, engulfed in the crowd's noise, there was the fly-half calmly hunting the best, flattest piece of turf from which to slot his kick. He realised he may not get another crack at the posts, he needed to make it count.

Lightning fast, he was weighing up his options. Where would the French come at him from? Which foot should he use? When would he have enough time? Like a sniper, he was finding the clearest, most secure line towards his target. Precision was the key, and it carried the night for an England team that has turned its fortunes around in the most remarkable of fashions.

Three weeks ago we had written them off – today they will fear no one. England's players have an air of confidence that comes with winning. They know that if they can weather the storm the opposition will put them under, then get their hit-man near the posts, he will pull the trigger and they can beat any side out there.

This is massive. The team have gelled and looking into their faces you knew they would go through hell and high water to back each other up. Once you have that, then you can almost start to dream the most impossible.

Other factors have also contributed to propel the English into the final, not least the resurgence of Mike Catt. Old he may be, but he has brought stability to the back line, and he gives Wilkinson a bit of a breather with his kicking and organisation.

Andy Gomarsall has been playing the games of his life, shifting the ball quickly away from the breakdown, probing with kicks and knowing when to harass the opposition scrum-half without breaking up England's defensive patterns. In the pack, Lewis Moody's willingness to put his body on the line sums up the team's attitude and grit, while Ben Kay is back to his best form in the line-out.

Players who come off the bench are making an impact. Joe Worsley made what had to be one of the best tackles in history. But this England team is not about individuals, even though one of them hogs the headlines. This is a team built around a squad where everyone plays a part, even the masseur.

With the game hanging by a thread at 5-9, England were awarded a penalty and Wilkinson steps up. Hang on though – a problem emerges with the ball, the seam is raised and bulging, and he wants another one, the first rejected as a tennis player rejects a ball when searching for the perfect serve.

The ballboy tosses one over, but up chirps Richard Wegrzyk, one of the busiest and finest men in the world. Masseur, acupuncturist, water carrier, training partner, he has many talents, not least of which is being eagle-eyed.

And on Saturday he may just have saved England. He spotted that the ball Wilkinson was going to use for the vital penalty was not one of the numbered match balls, not one of the balls that had been broken in by both sets of kickers in the build-up to the game. He shouted as much, Wilkinson heard, had a look and asked the ballboy to get him one of the numbered ones he had practised with. This made all the difference and the kick sailed over.

Had it not been for precision and teamwork, the outcome could have been very different. Instead, England have a chance to defend their championship and it suddenly looks like the sanest thing in the world.

The longest day

The day of the final is the longest a rugby player can experience. Remember all those times at school when you had an afternoon exam – how you looked at your books, put them away, looked at your books, put them away? How time never seemed to tick? Well multiply that by a hundred and then add some more for good measure.

Today for the England team will be interminable. There will be a late breakfast, body clocks tuned in to the 9 p.m. start (8 p.m. BST). The kickers may head out on to a pitch hoping to find some rhythm. The forwards will find a car park, or any sort of turf, for some line-outs. Mark Regan will throw a few – Simon Shaw and Ben Kay will catch a few, any excuse to get out of your room.

Lunch can't come fast enough. Then bed or a film, anything that takes your mind off the match, anything to conserve emotional energy.

You can play the game too many times in your head, and while psychology is important, running through all possible scenarios for 14 hours straight before the biggest game of your life is not the best way forward.

The mindset will be crucial in the match, but it also needs to help during the day controlling a player's heart rate and limiting their anxiety. So sleep, sleep. Then it is up again around four-ish, late afternoon.

Eat again; only you won't really eat as the butterflies are back. The fear is taking hold. Call it the buzz if you want, rename it to get rid of any negative thoughts but it is the same thing. Food is pushed around the plate as your mind fills with thoughts of the game. Imagine your first touch, your first tackle.

Then finally, at about 6.30, it is almost over. It is time to meet. There is nothing more to be said by the coaches, their time is up. Barring a substitution here, a replacement there, it is the players who now decide where the cup goes.

Climb aboard the bus. Nowhere is the trip to the stadium enjoyed more than in France. In the UK, the police escort sit in the traffic in front of you, waiting for gaps, easing through traffic. In France, police batons, boots, fists beat the cars out of the way.

Then suddenly, you see it, Stade de France, the stadium that, for good or bad, will forever play an enormous role in the players' lives. Will it be the stadium they transport themselves to whenever they need a happy memory, or will it be the one that will forever hold regrets?

The bus descends into the depths of the stadium, into darkness. A short walk to the changing room and you are free of the mental burden, of the expectation. Now all you want is for the clock to slow, time racing. You want to absorb everything, afraid that it will be over before you know it and you will hate not remembering every detail.

Before you know it you will be out on the pitch. Jonny Wilkinson will be in a zone. Phil Vickery will afford a smile and a handshake. Brian Ashton will enjoy a chat. The non-playing squad members will have the cameras out, the camcorders recording, wishing they were involved but hoping their mates can carry them home.

Then you look up and it's 90 minutes to go, and it does not seem long enough to get ready. You are further down the ankle-strapping queue than you would have liked, one of your studs is stuck and you can't change it. Where did you put your gum shield – side pocket or boot carrier?

The post-match suit comes out and is hung up. Damn, the shirt has creased and after you made a real effort to pack it well. The queue for the ankle strapping is still long. You need a pee. Jonny has been out kicking for 20 minutes, you are still in your underpants.

The defence coach wanders around, gentle reminders on Habana, du Preez, Burger. The front row never more than an inch away from each other – they know what awaits them and they had better be close all night.

Handshakes and hugs go on all night at every available opportunity. You need to feel, you need to touch, you need to know it is really happening and not some fantastic dream.

Finally it's your turn for strapping. Silence as the physio applies the tape and we realise that our bodies will have to pay the price for this most brutal and beautiful of days and sports. Hop off the massage table, a big inhale of smelling salts to clear the passages and kick-start your head, perhaps a can of caffeine drink.

The boys come together and with 30 minutes to go some words from Vickery. All the time Andy Gomarsall will have been talking, chivvying. Everyone searches for eye contact; every discussion is eyeball to eyeball. Look deep into your friend's soul; know he feels the same, that he will give everything for his team and country.

The warm-up on the pitch, the frightening intensity of it. Hit tackle pads, tell yourself that whatever comes down your channel will have to snap off your arms to get past.

You are a raging fire, your body is virtually uncontrollable, you simply do not know what to do with it. Your mind must then kick in and control the fury. Clear decisions and iron discipline must direct this human weapon.

In the background the teams are announced to the stadium and the noise is almost unbearable. The roar when Jonny's name and picture go on the big screen is both scary and comforting. Deafened, you go back in.

For some, a quick wave to friends and family, an acknowledgement that what you are about to do is as much for them and what they have given to you, what they have sacrificed for you, as it is about your team.

And then the changing room one last time. Final hugs that would crush a normal person, final words from the skipper imploring you simply to give everything you have. The normality of the final pee – the body still has to do its business when you would think that would be the last thing on your mind.

Then the referee's knock and the long walk. Face to face with the opposition in the tunnel. The final steps on to the field. A sudden surge of noise that lifts the hair off your head. It has arrived, the time is now. The day you thought would never end is almost over, and the moment you have dreamt of is upon you.

True class

South Africa have the bearing of champions. The night after they won the World Cup final, the Springboks were guests of honour at the International Rugby Board's annual dinner in Paris. You would have thought they might have been a bit dishevelled. They could have been forgiven for rolling in a bit wobbly, tired and emotional from their exertions from the night before. Nothing could have been further from the truth.

They were immaculate, controlled and worthy winners of the sport's ultimate trophy. Among the crowd at the dinner were some of rugby's greats. Men like JPR Williams and Gerald Davies. They were amazed by the size of the South Africans, awe-struck by the speed with which the game and the players' physicality has moved on.

Yet even though it is a thoroughly modern game, old-school values were on show and the Springboks took time to talk to all of the former players when they were approached. Ten minutes, sometimes 20 were kindly given. Critics of the South Africans talk of arrogance, of a self-belief that often grates. There was nothing like that on show. In fact there was very little behaviour that would have given away that the team had just beaten the very best that the world had to offer over a period of six weeks.

Occasionally, one of the players would break into a couple of bars of the Basque anthem that has been played at many of the grounds this tournament. But that really was it. The team were humble and dignified. When Bryan Habana was crowned player of the year, and compared to Jonah Lomu, he begged to differ. Lomu was a legend, a one-off; Habana was just a wing with a bit of gas.

This modesty was evident in the way South Africa approached their games in the tournament. They were a team in which everyone knew their place, how they fitted into that plan and what was required of them. However, they could also cover for the man standing next to them. If you want to see what the biggest change to rugby has been over the past few years, it is that players can now do a little bit of anything. It is not enough for the front five to get down and scrummage, or jump in the line-out. They now have to be able to run, pass and kick.

Did you see the massive South African Victor Matfield putting in crossfield kicks? A few years ago, he would have been laughed off the park. Now the old man of the Boks' pack, Os du Randt, is happy to find himself face-to-face with a young centre in the final moments of the game and tackle him without a problem. I doubt Scott Gibbs would bounce du Randt now as he did a few years ago.

Skills have been merged, and the South African side have been among the leaders in opening the game up. But they have done so by marrying this willingness to play an expansive game with discipline.

In the past, Butch James was often so hot-headed that he would lose his grip on the match. Now he is a cool customer who plays his game, directing the team with calm authority.

This calm steel runs through the team and nowhere is it more evident than in their mop-haired centre, the crazily youthful Francois Steyn. He backs himself when most of us would question the sanity of the decision. You could see his confidence when he teed up the penalty that all but took the game out of England's reach. The team knew he would hit it, you could see from their shoulders. Control yourself and control the game.

South Africa knew what they had to do and did it with icy precision. They backed their discipline, not giving away penalties that they knew Jonny Wilkinson would kick. Keep him out of the game and they would win. Keep to the plan, stay together and it was within their grasp.

On the field they had the backbone to win under extreme pressure. Off it, their shirt buttons were done up, their ties on straight, shoes polished. They looked like a team who were proud of what they had achieved. In short, they looked like world champions.

New Zealand 2011

*The 2011 World Cup was all about New Zealand. Would they
manage to shake the curse of the past 24 years and finally lift
the trophy on their home soil? Or would they choke again? For
England the tournament was full of hope and expectations.
Under their manager Martin Johnson they were a side growing
in confidence with enough talent to get to the knockout stages
and be a real problem to whichever team they met. No one
could have predicted just how wrong it would all go, one boozy
night souring the tournament for the whole squad and nation.
In the end this negative was outshone by New Zealand's victory
over France, finally letting a rugby-mad nation celebrate having
a team of worthy world champions.*

England have the brawn but have they got the brain?

The best rugby has a fluidity to it, an almost musical beat. England's problem is that they still love banging away like Animal on his *Muppet Show* drum-kit instead of finding a natural rhythm.

There is no doubt they still have the raw, brutal athletic power that gets Twickenham tub-thumping. Against Wales last week the trademarks of England's game were evident across the field; nasty at scrum time, heavy in the hit, deep in the lung. There was a sense of inevitability leading up to James Haskell's try as England turned the screw and forced tackle after tackle.

Then we saw the raw power of Manu Tuilagi after a good team build-up as the young man showed off his ferocity and crashed over under the sticks. The scoreboard ticked over with dropped goals. It was not beautiful, but it was everything you could want from a team.

And yet for all the right decisions that were made, all the text-book calls, there were elements that worry me as we head towards the Rugby World Cup.

I am not talking of dropped balls or poor passes. The best way to get to the heart of the problem is to look at the defence. This is an area where most of the thinking is black and white. Patterns are run, rules need to be followed, positions filled. Yet for all the rigidity, if players cannot freestyle, if they cannot go with the flow, if they cannot, for want of a better phrase and I hate myself for writing it, play jazz rugby, then they will never shut teams out.

The first Welsh try was a perfect example. Wales were attacking the England line on the left side of the field. If the ball came out quickly then England's wide men had no chance. But the ball was slow – very slow.

It was so slow that the attack should have been snuffed out. What England should have done is re-form, slide out one. They should have heard the call from wide and moved. It didn't happen.

Rhys Priestland must have been hoarse shouting for the ball and yet England continued to stand still in a tight group. To their credit, when they did react, when the ball was shifted wide by Wales, they moved with good, aggressive line speed. But again they needed to be more aware, more willing to look past 'the right thing to do'.

As the ball flew down the Wales line, the textbook says England's defenders needed to come out and make a tackle. When you are so close to your line you do not let a man run. Follow the textbook and Delon Armitage was right to step in and tackle Morgan Stoddart.

Unfortunately, the textbook is wrong. What Armitage should have done was close the space but not commit, so putting indecision in the opposition's mind and giving the cover time to arrive. Riki Flutey had worked his socks off inside and would have made it across to tackle Stoddart if only Armitage had chilled on the outside.

It is not daft to hold and then shift to the outside five yards from your own line. It takes guts and confidence in your team. Quade Cooper and Dan Carter want to turn defenders into jumpers, not chillers – men who panic and dive in are easy pickings. In the end, Stoddart got his pass away and George North scored with Flutey all over him like a cheap suit. Having worked so hard on the inside Flutey nearly made it to North, never mind Stoddart.

That is athleticism and guts. Shame that what England really needed was a little more sang froid. It is what will get them through the toughest encounters and will make the difference in the World Cup knockout stages. Ask yourself if New Zealand would have leaked a try.

England need to tweak their game. They need to find some subtlety to go with their power. Take North's second try. The lead-up saw Haskell against Sam Warburton. Haskell is the supreme athlete desperate to prove himself as a world-class player. Warburton, I think, is already there. As the ball went right to left on the Welsh side, Haskell had his man lined up. But as the ball drifted in the Twickenham air to Warburton, a feint of the hips, an arc down the line of the flight of the ball and Haskell was left flat-footed staring inwards. Moments later North crashed over.

You sometimes wish that Haskell, like England, would not work so hard. Haskell has done everything to get the most out of his body, he understands and is aware of his weaknesses and works hard to disguise them. It's just sometimes you wish he spent less time in the gym and on contact, and a little more on reading the game and understanding space and how to exploit it.

This is England's challenge today, not just as players but as team and management. Over the next four weeks, they cannot get much fitter. Instead, they should focus on getting more natural and fluid.

They need to speed up their reactions to a break and become more in tune to where the next threat is coming from. They need to fight their instinct to return to organisational rugby and have the guts to set off in one direction with pace and conviction and know that someone will be there to help out.

That sharpness of brain is the final barrier that England must overcome if they are to persuade more than just the faithful that they are genuine World Cup contenders.

Game changers

The Fosbury Flop, the Doosra, the triple salko, the Vardon Grip, William Webb Ellis, serve and volley. A list of people and techniques that have been game changers. For the generations that witnessed their achievements it must have seemed as if they were defying gravity, rewriting rules, bucking trends that were unbuckable. A unique moment that became the norm. After last Saturday, when Ireland beat Australia, we have another couple of names to add to the list of innovators and executions of the improbable.

The man is Les Kiss, Ireland's defensive coach; the move is the Choke Tackle.

Like the best ideas, the theory is simple. Under modern rugby laws if a ball is held up in a maul scenario then the attacking team lose the ball, the defenders get given the put-in at a scrum. That is the best-case scenario.

The worst is that the attackers keep the ball but have to commit more players to winning it, slowing them down and thinning out their options across the field. This, to the smart mind of Mr Kiss, was a loophole to be taken advantage of. Once spotted it was all about getting the idea put into practice. Again this is down to the evolution of sport, and could not have happened until rugby was professional.

For the Choke to work, players need the physical strength to be able to hold the opposition up in the tackle, maintain their feet and stay upright despite being hit hard by scrambling attackers who see their possession is under threat.

A decade ago, the Choke would not have worked. The gym monkeys finally have their uses, not least because much of the technique we learnt as children now needs to be ignored.

There is a third way

The truth that any player, no matter how big, will fall over if you hit them low enough still rings true, and it is central to the two most used tackles.

First there is the classic tackle. Hips low, head up, eyes on the opponent's legs. Then comes the dip, the thrust into contact, the shoulder into the thigh, the head placed on the backside, the snap of the arms, the leg drive, the small lift. Do it right and the attacker hits the ground and the defender can get back on their feet and compete for the ball.

Second, there is the double tackle, invented to stop the ball being offloaded to support runners. For this to work, the first man adopts the classic tackle from the inside, going low. The second defender steps in from the outside and goes high, not head high but chest high, and closes around the ball as the attacker is going to ground.

When it works, no offload is made, a mass of bodies end up on the deck and a new defensive line can be put into place around the fresh breakdown. Very effective and a variation on the concept of getting a player to the deck, quickly.

The Choke tackle goes against this because it redefines what you are trying to do to the ball carrier. The Choke is all about keeping the ball carrier on his feet. It goes against everything we have been told.

Use your visualisation techniques to see it in action. The Choke requires two men. Extras can join the maul once a successful Choke has been made, but the initial move needs two players.

It also needs an unbelievably well-organised defensive plan and super-fit players committed to getting the line ready and manned enough in order for the Choke to become an option.

From phase play it is extremely difficult but not impossible as O'Brien, Ferris and O'Connell showed so beautifully. But the Choke is really at its best from set-piece play and particularly line-out play. The classic line-out attacking options tend to come from an off-the-top quick ball aimed at sending a big man over the gain line, allowing the attacking team to play off the quick ruck ball, offload out of the tackle, get in behind defenders and move at pace.

The best way to stop this is to go after the attackers' big man, their line breaker. And as with any big animal, it's always best to lay a trap.

How does the Choke work?

In the Choke tackle, the inside defender wants to have a slightly offset stance allowing them to throw their weight into the tackle at a ten o'clock or two o'clock angle.

The key is not to be straight on. This is not about symmetry, you don't want the tacklers directly opposite the attacker because that doesn't allow the second defender to get involved. You need to leave a gap to lure the ball carrier further forward. You want him to keep running, you want the attacker to think he has a hole to attack. It's the classic mug's alley. All the attacker sees is the half chance, ignoring the double trouble closing in on either side of him.

As the attacker advances, the defenders come together, the hole closes. The tackler who is closest to the ball-carrying arm of the attacker goes low, but not so low that he puts the runner down. Instead he hits on an upward angle, trying to get his shoulder under the ball, keeping it high, keeping the centre of gravity high.

The defender on the non-ball-carrying arm goes chest high. He drives the shoulder into the ball and makes sure it is going nowhere, suspended animation, clamped between his arms, the shoulder of the other defender and chest of the attacker. A very, very difficult place to get the ball out of.

The tackler who attacked lower down is now in charge of maintaining the stability of the maul, using tremendous leg and upper-arm strength. The man on the ball also works on stability but his major role is to be a clamp. His other role is to make sure that when things come to a halt then the attacker is turned away from his support players, giving the ref an easy decision to make.

No chance of the ball coming out quickly? Whistle blown, scrum, defending side ball.

And how Ireland made it work

The first time Ireland used the Choke against Australia there were 32 seconds on the clock. It was an Australian line-out, nothing too odd at first glance with seven players against seven and a hooker throwing in. But if you look closely at Ireland you realise that they had no scrum-half in the standard sense of the position.

There was no player one yard from the line-out waiting for the ball. And the hooker who usually covers the front of the line-out was actually standing in the main part of it. In fact, Ireland's normal scrum-half was standing where the hooker usually goes. Which means a forward who should have been part of the line-out was awol.

267

This escapee was Sean O'Brien, the giant mobile outhouse from Leinster. He, along with Keith Earls, the blindside winger, were standing in the midfield where they thought the opposition would attack. Ireland packed this area to bursting.

So when Australia sent McCabe up the middle, he stood no chance. The Choke tackle was actioned by O'Brien and Earls, the ball won back in the form of a scrum, Irish put-in. There were risks if the ball came out, there was space elsewhere. But it didn't matter because Ireland were making a statement, and it was one that Australia chose to ignore to their cost.

Five times the Irish executed the Choke, and five times the scrum feed went to the dominant Irish pack. The scrums won Ireland penalties and points. The match was Ireland's thanks to the Choke.

It was a technique that defined a game and may well have changed the course of a World Cup. Clubs across the world will be trying to copy it, coaches trying to nullify and implement it. There's no doubt it will have an effect. And while it may be too early to add the Choke and Les Kiss to the list of legends, what I do know is I will never forget where I saw it put into practice so perfectly.

The auld enemy

Emotions confuse things. You can't legislate for feelings. And this is why Scotland are such a dangerous team. They believe they can beat England.

I know how fervent they are because I had a midnight beer with their coach just before the World Cup. It was far too late and Andy Robinson and I were in a hotel bar chatting about life with a heavy rugby accent. He would not entertain the thought that Scotland could lose to England. It did not register as an option. What struck me most was that this was not beer-fuelled bravado. It was a stone-cold sober sense of destiny for his team.

They have been thinking about this game ever since the draw was made. Forget that they lost to Argentina. If they win they can still send England home. The maths is more complicated than it needs to be, the reality much simpler; win the match, add it all up later.

So be prepared to see a Scotland who throw everything they have at England. It will not be pretty.

This is when the desperation of the knockout stages sets in. It's the time you get the sneaky feeling, right at the very back of your mind, that it can all end at any moment. It's when you realise the very real implication that an average 80 minutes will mean a boarding pass and an early flight no matter how great a warrior you are.

Try as you might to focus on the positives, it's impossible not to at least acknowledge these nervy thoughts in the run-up to the game. Keeping these fears in check will be one of England's biggest challenges. For Scotland they will be the fire that drives them on.

While I think the emotions of this game will be harder to handle, England look well placed. The psychology of this England team has always been about getting to October 1 with a fit and healthy squad. By and large they have achieved that. There have been problems with the breakdown, there have been injury scares, headline-grabbing boozing sessions and controversial incidents regarding their ball selection.

But against Romania there were signs that the team were coming together. Lovely width, better precision. Lewis Moody was epic when going for 50-50 balls on the floor. His crazy desire to get on the deck and win the ball as an out and out No 7 will be crucial both today and if England progress.

As a pack, England's forwards were starting to look more comfortable in attack. And while I have questioned James Haskell's ball-playing ability in the past, I have to commend him for his distribution against Romania, helping create a couple of tries. Mike Tindall was excellent at the breakdown again with turnovers. There was a lot of work off the ball, which is good to see because in sudden-death matches it's often what you do without the ball that wins you tight ties. Manu Tuilagi is a game breaker, give him the ball a lot. He sucks people in, he beats people, he gets his team over the gain line with a step or a bump or a burst of speed.

England's line-out was exceptional and it was a tough call to bring Courtney Lawes back in for Tom Palmer. However, there were still some worrying areas for England. The counter-rucking was poor at times, and players were knocked off the ball by the Romanians. This is one area where England need to be nastier, because Scotland will fly into all areas of contact. It will all be about control, which is why, as good as Haskell has been, I spot a weakness with him playing at No 8.

The error count is too high when Haskell plays there and this is an area that can be targeted. Not least because when the pressure is on and the mind starts to race, the points start to get squeezed, the fingers will also tighten and close down just that little bit. And England don't want that, especially as they will be playing outdoors for the first time this tournament.

So far England have been inside the Otago greenhouse. Very little wind, no rain to mess with their game plan. Scotland have been out in the elements. England's bodies and brains will take time to adjust to the change.

The clock is ticking, the charge to the final starts here, and neither side want to be left standing.

England have to believe they can play and win four games in 22 days, defying the odds and the doubters. Scotland need to buy into their coach's evangelical belief that their World Cup is not over and produce the game of their lives. In the end it will all come down to who wants it the most.

It is time England go for it with everything they've got

Bob Dwyer, the great Australia and Leicester coach, once told me that there is no such thing as a bad decision on a rugby field. What matters is how you and your team-mates react to it. If you go hard at it, if you commit, and if your pals back you up, then it will normally be OK. What kills a team is not bad decisions but a lack of decisions. At their worst against Scotland last week, England's decision-making was deafening in its silence.

In the first half everything was slowed down to a crawl, it turned into an arm wrestle and looked as if England were terrified, afraid of risking a loss rather than willing to chance a win. Where was the tap and go from free kicks given at scrums or line-outs? Where was the willingness to move the ball quickly and wide? The one-dimensional runners that we saw early on against Scotland could have been defended by a pub team. And while England are good at

271

squeezing the life out of a game, at some point an opponent will take their chance.

That's why England need to be much more positive against France. They have to get on the front foot and make sure they don't face death by a thousand kicks at the hands of Dimitri Yachvili and Morgan Parra, whose feet are rapier sharp. The one thing in England's favour is that as bad as they have been, France have been worse. And they still have another chance to play, to show the world they can mix it with the best.

It must be a bitter pill for sides such as Scotland and Samoa to swallow, yet the simple truth is that England are still in the competition. Complain all you want about the fortune of the draw, bemoan your luck as a southern hemisphere side that you are surrounded by much tougher world-ranking opposition, it's just that there is every chance that one of these two underperforming teams will stay in the tournament all the way to the final weekend.

And in the past 12 months, despite their problems so far this World Cup, England have shown they can live with and beat some of the best teams in the world. Australia at Twickenham, Wales in Cardiff, Ireland in Dublin. These are not easy matches to win, and while critics may point out the glorious troughs, it won't make the peaks just disappear.

And that is what England must focus on now – reproducing that form in a one-off game, striving to accentuate the positives and banish thoughts of their mediocrity. Some of England's issues have been fixed by selection, the rest, and way more important, must come from a change of attitude. The team must go at the French with vibrancy and pace. It's not time for sevens rugby, but there must be an injection of speed and quick thinking. England have poachers and try-scorers.

Chris Ashton is as sharp as any and in the midfield they have a weapon in Manu Tuilagi. He could make it into any team in this tournament bar New Zealand. They need to be brought into the game. Tuilagi at line-outs, with off-the-top ball. It's not rocket science. Just give the kid the ball and from the resulting quick ruck, this guy does not produce slow ball, Ashton should be brought in floating around the rucks off the shoulder of the No 9 or the No 10. This is where he is lethal for Northampton and can be deadly for England. Ben Youngs must tap and go, tap and go. Bury the wavering French who stand on the edge.

England have an improving platform at the scrum, and Nick Easter at the base will help. The man is a rock and picture of serenity when the ball is bobbling around. The line-out work in the second half got much better, with Tom Croft outstanding and Tom Palmer adding from the bench, Palmer had to start. The aerial battle in the damp was extremely sound, and Ben Foden and Delon Armitage were quick to help each other out when a mistake was made, Mark Cueto will not weaken here. Fear not.

Jonny Wilkinson has always talked of making it to where he is today due to the unwavering faith in him from those who matter. This is the ultimate test of faith from manager Martin Johnson. I am not concerned about the goal-kicking, no one else I would rather have to take the match-winning penalty. But we must see Toulon Jonny not English Jonny. Go and play. Stand flatter, take early balls, avoid contact, keep it moving, half break, offload. They are all in the locker.

And most importantly, the French are utterly terrified of you. Jog around them in the warm-up, big smile, say bonsoir and watch them crumble. I know he is not a tart or a thesp but he has to play his trump card. Positive early outlook, rugged teak defence, and the man you want on the field in the closing stages, Wilkinson, ready to take his shot no matter how messy it has been so far. Flood must be himself. He is a top-class 12. Absolutely top class 12. This is a bold move. A good move. A change of attitude move. Defence is no issue for the lad. The left and right foot at 10 and 12. The added dimension of width in the midfield will make Tuilagi more dangerous and Foden more active. A further plus for England was that their discipline got much better in the second half, and turnovers and penalties started to turn the game.

At the same time, getting themselves out of a hole at 3-12 is not to be underestimated. And this is what England must focus on. All their good stuff came when the pace and intensity were lifted. Sucking the life out of a game with no intent or pace takes the game to a dogfight. I hope England have been honest, have been brutal, have understood their limitations. Yet I also hope they have maintained their seemingly limitless supply of belief, Johnson's greatest legacy to this team, because they've played four and won four and are in the quarter-finals again.

Right or wrong, it doesn't matter. They are where they want to be and it is time they went for it with everything they've got.

Will Wales or France reach the final?

Key battles where I thought the northern hemisphere semi-final would be won and lost:

Jamie Roberts v Aurélien Rougerie

Roberts has been magnificent, and sums up Wales's new levels of fitness. Look at his carry close to the Ireland line in the opening seconds last week: Donncha O'Callaghan, a second row who understands the importance of the goal-line tackle, stands in his way. Roberts takes his moment, charges past team-mates to make the carry and then – bam! The contact is won. O'Callaghan's head rattles, spit flies, a gum shield is ejected high into the sky. Roberts was making a statement. Against him for France will be Rougerie, a man who picked up a horrific injury close to the tournament and really has no right to be playing. But warriors do what they have to do. The Clermont captain is, by definition, a leader of men. France's mercurial coach, Marc Lièvremont, has put little men in his back line to dance and to score, but for them to get the space, they need a rock in midfield and Rougerie is that rock. He will be ordered to get in among bodies, enforce the breakdown and make it a dogfight in the wide channels.

Sam Warburton v Thierry Dusautoir

The captains, both of whom have been involved in great quarter-final wins. Both France v New Zealand in 2007 and Wales v Ireland in 2011 were classic rearguard actions that will have taught them how to win when it matters most. In terms of skill and ability,

Warburton is as good as anyone. Give me a name from the best –
Richie McCaw, Heinrich Brussow, David Pocock, Sean O'Brien –
and he loses nothing. He is young and fearless.

He is a man you want to follow, much like his scary French
counterpart, Dusautoir. Remember Dusautoir's eyes as he led his
team out against England? A stare devoid of emotion, acknowledg-
ing no one, focusing on what he was about to do. In that moment
you understood what faced England. And, perhaps the best compliment you can pay any back-row forward, he reminded me of
Richard Hill. He gets all over the field, and still makes sure that
when he does arrive it counts. A tackle, a turnover, a counter-ruck,
a drive; there are no wasted contributions.

Adam Jones v Nicolas Mas

Mas is a symbol of the scrummaging heart that beats so powerfully
in French rugby. He is the guy who must set the tone and who will
allow the backs to move wide and fast. Ball-carrying is not his skill;
if anything, it is a distraction to the main event: the scrum and
driving maul.

Opposite him will be Adam Jones, a man whose form has never
really deviated.

Injuries to him have cost Wales victories. Wales have always been
able to play but they have not always had the steady, squared-off
platform that the scrum can provide. Without it, launching the
backs becomes harder.

Jones is the missing link of Welsh rugby.

Defensive systems

Both sides ask questions that very few other international sides
pose and, as a result, both will have to adjust very quickly. The
Welsh defence has been epic and a team who know they can tackle

and hold out against incredible pressure are difficult to beat. But the French are a very different animal. They move the point of attack much better than almost any other side. Wales can tackle and be brave. Can they now read, shift and realign quickly enough to deal with France? For Les Bleus, the challenge is much the same: they must find a way of keeping their line when Wales try to inject the pace and rhythm they have.

Control from No 10

The merry-go-round of fly-halves goes on. Huge blow to Wales with the withdrawal of Rhys Priestland. James Hook must now pick up the baton, stay true to what has got them here and get the centres, Roberts and Davies, who've looked world beaters with Priestland, in behind the defence.

France's Morgan Parra is a scrum-half, but he has the nerve of a gambler and is there to bring his back three into play with the width of his passing. Parra lacks the experience and Hook has had questions over his game management. The one that adapts and makes the best choices will swing the balance of the match.

Prediction

I got it wrong last week, because I backed England with my heart and not my head. So this week I should give in to the nagging feeling I have about France. But then I get flooded by memories of a stadium, an anthem, a history that has yearned for this moment. So, Wales, do you mind if I join you today? My lot weren't much good.

That still second of invincibility

Stare into the eyes of an All Black during the Haka and you see a deep cold darkness. Some will say its nothing more than adrenalin-dilated pupils. Others will tell you it's a trick of the light. The foolish will claim it's a hint of nerves. They are all wrong.

What you glimpse is a man's soul and it draws you in. As the challenge of the Haka is thrown down you find yourself tumbling into a stare like Alice down the rabbit hole. The noise of the crowd disappears and your mind fills with the deafening voice of a nation asking you one very simple question: 'These boys will do whatever it takes to win. How far are you willing to go?' And in that moment, on that field, no matter how you got there, you have to decide. What are your limits, where do you draw the line, how much pain can you endure?

Last week, during the semi-final Haka, you could feel the pulse that has been driving this country's team. The crowd stamped their feet and joined in, the stadium's two temporary stands moved to their beat, swaying with intent and the implied threat and danger. The players fed the crowd with their display of togetherness and the crowd fed the team with a power surge of support.

I doubt I will witness anything like it ever again. This was 24 years of pain and hurt bubbling and simmering. This was the understanding that since 1987 it has been a pretty thankless task being an All Black supporter.

The desperation to make the final was palpable on the streets of Auckland before the match, with no enjoyment or excitement about the game ahead just a desire to fast-forward time. They knew they were on the cusp of a moment that could change their collective history. The irony is that should they go all the way – and New Zealand supporters already seem to be doing a mental lap of honour – then for all its life-changing impact there is a very good chance the players won't remember too much about the final.

You remember the lead-up, you remember the hours spent turning yourselves into machines, working on skills, your fitness, developing independence of thought but within a team with a natural leader, tempered by knowledge that comes from playing for a coach who is not afraid to leave people out if needs be. Ruthless. Every bead of sweat, each repetition, all those quiet nights reminding you that a World Cup is not about the will to win it's about being willing to prepare for victory.

This New Zealand team have earned this moment, they have been on their emotional and mental journey. I played against Ma'a Nonu in his first cap in 2003 and his transformation as a player beautifully tracks the development of the current team. First time round he was a flat-track bully who could only see one way to win and that was by going straight through or over the opposition. Today he can do it all. He can slide down passes, change his lines, pop up in unexpected places, offload deftly, if he has to, go at it like a bull in a china shop.

The team around him has also developed balance and they have options to win a game four different ways. This understanding has allowed them to carry different styles of player but all with one goal in mind – being error free, building pressure, taking chances, keeping the grip applied to their opponents' collective throat.

Cruden banging over a drop goal was a final acknowledgement of everything they had earlier hated about rugby and the view that sometimes taking three points will suffice. If France are going to have any chance against this stranglehold then they will need to find their own sense of unity which seems to have eluded them for much of this tournament. Fractured and flailing I wrote them off well before the final. I have learnt my lesson. They can be dangerous but only if they can find calm in the midst of the battle.

When France lose their heads, they lose their games. They beat Wales not with emotion but with a death squeeze that was almost English in its lack of imagination and dumb reliance on kicking. Against New Zealand they will have to play out of their skins and conquer their fears. And before the macho among you start shouting that the French don't feel fear, let me tell you this – every changing room knows fear. It will be in with Les Bleus and the All Blacks. Courage is not a lack of fear. It is having the strength to feel it and still go out there and do what is needed.

World Cups are won by teams that can look around their changing room and have that one quiet moment, that one second when they know beyond any shadow of any doubt that they are among friends who will stand by them no matter what. Their time will come when the coaches have left and the subs are waiting in the tunnel, when the door shuts and only the 15 stand together, cocooned from the hysteria building outside. Their captain will walk into the middle of the changing room, the huddle forming round him for that team moment, the tactile bond by its very nature reassuring, the feeling of togetherness, of safety in numbers, the primeval urge to stay together believing everything will be alright. There will be a rattle of studs on the floor as this mass of bodies sways one way and then the other, the smaller men shunted by the silverbacks, the huddle moving like a wave back and forth as the hugs come and are then released. The smell of sweat and musty muscle cream, no great speeches, only the promise from the skipper to leave the field a winner. Then the silence again, the hugs and the look, *that look,* from every single player. It has to come from 1 to 15 and if they get it right it will never be forgotten.

When I am asked what I remember about my World Cup final, this is the moment I always mention. The match itself I have never watched. My mental picture is only flashes of action; the tackle missed on Mortlock I can't deny; the knock-on in the Australian 22 that will not disappear. Yet I can't remember much else except for that moment in the changing room, that still second of invincibility, of knowing that right there, right then, I would not trade any one of our players no matter who was offered. It was a beautiful feeling. The final will be very different, a fury of emotion, noise, speed and lightning quick incidents. If a player loses focus, if they forget their promise to their team and themselves, then they will fail. The only way they can win is to make sure that when their moment comes they stare straight back and never blink.

England 2015

Hosting a World Cup is a unique opportunity for a country to show how much it loves rugby. It can be the perfect host and provide the correct environment for the tournament. But it also needs to show how it will use the competition to develop and strengthen the game both at home and abroad. That is why I was so happy to be involved in England's ultimately successful bid for the 2015 World Cup. Not only could we put on the best possible show but we would promise a legacy that will reach far beyond England's borders. Putting this book together I was reminded how much the game of rugby has changed and grown over the past decade or so. From law changes to player payments, rugby has been morphing into one of the world's best spectator sports and I can't wait to see the game on show in England in 2015.

A legacy

This is the full extract of a speech I gave to the International Rugby Board in Dublin at the presentation of England's 2015 World Cup bid.

I want to talk about the legacy of our bid, and its impact on grassroots rugby.

I stand here as a Hopper and a Drummer. A Northern lad who learnt his rugby at Preston Grasshoppers and at Waterloo, I am a grassroots man, through and through, and I have seen the power of rugby and its ability to change lives on an individual level and on a community basis.

I stand before you as player, pundit and more recently a touchline dad. I have experienced the changing rooms of school, university and junior club level, and none of them were any different to the one I sat in, in Sydney, on November 22, 2003.

The same spirit, trust and dedication that saw England win that night, is seen in every changing room in every club on every Saturday. We hope on the back of our bid to allow more youngsters to experience this incredible feeling of unity.

Our sport needs fast guys, tall guys and strong guys. There is a role for every physique and every skill set. What better metaphor for an increasingly diverse world than the game of rugby football.

Because rugby is about the realisation that, no matter how great our differences, we all have to work as one team if we want to reach our goals, like no other sport rugby acknowledges that 'none of us is as good as all of us'.

Rugby is the fastest-growing major sport in England, up 40 per cent since 2003, we want to target a further 40 per cent over the next eight years. We want to broaden the base and increase the diversity of our young players. And we are committing to making sure every club has one new team by 2016 as our minimal aim.

The health of the nation is at the forefront of our bid. Over half of 11–14-year-olds in Britain now watch or play rugby once a month, keeping kids healthy and reducing obesity. It's not just the physical health, the mental health and moral well-being of being involved in such a wonderful sport are key too.

Our bid contains the outline of a schools and youth club programme to use the tournament to attract more kids to rugby and to sustain existing players in the sport. It is our aim to use the 2015 World Cup to reinforce the role of the grassroots rugby clubs, to be the arenas in which we will see health across the board improve and with that affect the very way in which children live their lives.

It is a huge focus of the World Cup bid to broaden the base of the game, for me of upmost importance rugby has the ability to change lives of those less fortunate or trying to regain their place in society. I have spent the last four months on a rugby pitch in North Wales with kids who have erred in their lives, be it drugs, crime or in some cases a simple lack of drive; and through the power of rugby I have watched these boys grow into men, and men I would be proud to have alongside me now. The project has reiterated what a difference we can make, and what giving England World Cup 2015 will give support to.

We have a once in a generation chance to deliver a lasting legacy, to reach out to new players and fans and to recruit a new generation to our game. Building on the government's decade of sport, we can deliver an elite tournament with a very mass appeal.

Rugby is about friendship, trust, second chances and the fighting spirit. And it's about the realisation that we all have to suffer and work as one team if we want to reach our goals, and the stark truth that none of us can make it on our own.

Our legacy will not just be to grow the playing, coaching and volunteer base for rugby football, but also to spread the values and beliefs of our very special game: teamwork, respect, discipline, friendship, the celebration of difference.

That would be quite some legacy.

England on a global stage

When the International Rugby Board announced in Dublin that England's bid to host the 2015 Rugby World Cup, a bid that I have been personally involved in, was successful, a range of emotions rushed through me.

Relief that our bid had been accepted by the IRB Council; excitement about what a festival of rugby England will host; humility at the honour we have been given to host the third-largest sporting event on the planet.

I also have to confess to feeling a little envy. It is not an emotion

I feel often. I have fulfilled many of my life's ambitions. I have won a Rugby World Cup winner's medal and have a great job and a wonderful family.

But I do envy those England players, and in fact all of those players who will now appear on the global stage at the home of English rugby, Twickenham, and a host of other iconic and world-renowned stadiums around the country.

To play at Wembley in the World Cup, the Emirates Stadium, St James' Park or even the 'Theatre of Dreams', Old Trafford, will be an experience of a lifetime and one that every player and supporter will remember as long as they live.

The reason is that not only do I know that England will host a commercially successful tournament, but I am even more certain it will be a passionate one that showcases the best of rugby union around the world.

We have committed to the IRB that we will host the most successful Rugby World Cup ever and for me that also means being the most vibrant, colourful and exuberant ever.

We in England have a vast supporter base and one that is possibly the most culturally diverse in the world. Every nation competing will have its own supporter base and the rest of England will contribute every step of the way.

That means every player will get to play in front of crowds of 30,000, 40,000 or even 50,000 – regardless of what country they play for. And they will do so in front of the fairest and most passionate rugby supporters in the world.

For that I envy them. But I have to admit I envy the English players the most. I know what it is like to win a World Cup on a balmy evening in Sydney but I will never know what it is like to have the opportunity to win a World Cup in front of my home crowd.

I was part of the England squad at the 1999 World Cup, when

we missed an opportunity to beat New Zealand in the pool match at Twickenham before we were smashed by South Africa in the quarter-final in Paris.

Former England players, such as Jason Leonard and Brian Moore, still talk about meeting the Queen in 1991 but ultimately failing to fulfil their dream in front of their home crowd at Twickenham in the final against Australia.

But I believe England will have a great opportunity to win the tournament in 2015.

Historically, the host country normally has an advantage and while the 2011 World Cup in New Zealand looks a daunting task for England – albeit one that Martin Johnson will attack head-on – the building blocks are already being put in place to have a real crack at it in 2015.

England got to the final of the Under-20 World Cup in 2011, losing to New Zealand, and it is that generation that will come through. And who's to say there isn't a World Cup final for them to win in 2015?

ACKNOWLEDGEMENTS

The *Daily Telegraph*, especially Keith Perry, Nick Keller and Lisa Norman of Benchmark Sport.

Ben Richardson, my trusted old housemate and back row friend, the greatest sounding board on the planet.